KIM
CAMPBELL

60 YEARS IN CANADA
19 33
19 93
HarperCollins

KIM CAMPBELL

The Making of a Politician

ROBERT FIFE

A Phyllis Bruce Book
HarperCollins*PublishersLtd*

First Edition

Canadian Cataloguing in Publication Data

Fife, Robert
Kim Campbell : the making of a politician

Includes index.
"A Phyllis Bruce book".
ISBN 0-00-255076-8

1. Campbell, Kim, 1947– .
2. Cabinet ministers — Canada — Biography.*
3. Politicians — Canada — Biography.
4. Progressive Conservative Party of Canada — Biography.
5. Women in politics — Canada — Biography.
I. Title.

FC631.C26F5 1993   971.064'7'092   C93-094489-5
F1034.3.C26F5 1993

93 94 95 96 97 98 99 ❖ HC 10 9 8 7 6 5 4 3 2 1

For Naomi R. Goldenberg, my partner in this project,
and for Natalie Goldenberg-Fife, our daughter

CONTENTS

ACKNOWLEDGMENTS

In late November 1992, my editor, Phyllis Bruce, and I rolled the dice and gambled that Brian Mulroney would depart and be succeeded by Kim Campbell. A month later, I telephoned Campbell at her Vancouver home to broach the subject of a biography. She thought the idea was "presumptuous" but nonetheless told me that she was willing to co-operate.

By the time Mulroney announced his resignation in February, Campbell's handlers had decided to keep her far away from me. Top aide Ray Castelli explained that I had a reputation for being a tough journalist who "could not be trusted." I took that to mean that I could not be trusted to write a laudatory book about his boss. He was right: I intended to write an objective account of Campbell's life and not a brochure for her campaign. Nevertheless, I hope that when Mr. Castelli reads this very unauthorized biography, he will agree that I have painted a balanced portrait of Ms. Campbell.

Since Kim's father, George Campbell, declined to be interviewed, I had to rely upon other journalists to whom he had granted interviews. I am grateful to four reporters who went out of their way to provide me with transcripts or tapes of their discussions with Mr. Campbell: Heather Bird of *The Ottawa Sun*; Stephen Brunt of *The Globe and Mail*; E. Kaye Fulton of *Maclean's* and Laura Lynch of CBC National Radio. Kaye, Stephen and Heather were also generous with their friendship and valuable insight.

Two other journalists helped me a great deal: Vaughn Palmer, political columnist with *The Vancouver Sun*, shared his knowledge about Campbell's years in the Victoria legislature; and Claire Hoy, author and free-lance columnist, gave me sage advice about how to proceed with writing a political biography. In addition, three books were immensely useful: *School Wars* by Crawford Kilian, *Fantasyland* by Gary Mason and Keith Baldrey, and *Fantasy Government* by Stan Persky. I recommend these sources to anyone interested in doing further research on Kim Campbell's stint on the Vancouver School Board and her time with the Socreds.

I appreciate the help I received from the staff of the National Archives, the Library of Parliament, the Vancouver Public Library and the libraries of Pacific Press. I am also grateful to the employees of the Vancouver School Board who made records available to me.

Some of the people whose knowledge and skills were of benefit to the book are: Bill Beckingham, Bill Bennett, Stephen Bindman, Sister Thelma Boutin, Stevie Cameron, Rachel Campbell, Mary Clancy, Lorenne Clark, Doug Cook, Michel Cormier, Shelagh Day, Ken Denike, Fred Drummie, Mike Duffy, Carol Gran, Charlotte Gray, Derik Hodgson, Kal Holsti, Bob Horner, Bob Jackson, Mary Janigan, Lyall Knott, Phyllis Leonardi, Kathleen Mahoney, Pat MacAdam, Sheila McIntyre, Gerard McNeil, Shirley McPhail, Cathy Morris, Don Mouton, Peter O'Neil, Bill Rodgers, Gillian Shaw, Elizabeth Sheehy, Bud Smith, Bill Vander Zalm, Ginny Vessey, David Vienneau, Phyllis Vroom, Ralph White, Bertha Wilson and Geoffrey York.

There are some people who cannot be named in these acknowledgments, but they know who they are and how much I appreciate their help.

I thank Paul Godfrey, president of The Toronto Sun Publishing Corporation, and Les Pyette, the *Sun's* corporate editor, for their encouragement. I also received support from *Sun* friends Bob McConachie, Sue Dewar, John Paton, Chuck and Betts Stapley and my colleagues in the Parliamentary Bureau: Sean Durkan, Michel Gratton, Angela Graves, Jan Lounder, Tim Naumetz and Peter Stockland.

A special note of appreciation to our neighbors, Shelley and Bill Taylor, for their assistance, and to the children of Fentiman Avenue for providing welcome distraction: Julia and Robin Campbell, Madeline and Duncan Macdonald, Laura and Matthew Floyd, Molly and Andrew Graves and Jessie Taylor.

This book could not have been written without the full-time assistance of Naomi Goldenberg, my partner in life and throughout this project. She helped me with my research, spent countless hours reworking and reshaping the copy and offered thoughtful advice both as a feminist and an astute political analyst. Our daughter, Natalie, was often neglected while we worked. We thank her for her patience and maturity. Now that the book is finished we promise to take her to watch the Ottawa Lynx.

MAKING HISTORY

"Come on, then!" roared the Queen, and Alice joined the
procession, wondering very much what would happen next.

— *Lewis Carroll*

Kim Campbell's life is not the stuff of fairy tales. The stories
we often tell ourselves about the men and women who stand
at the forefront of national consciousness do not apply to our
nineteenth prime minister. Campbell cannot be depicted in the
same way as a male hero who follows a difficult but fairly straight-
forward path to wealth and influence with a beautiful maiden at
his side. Nor can she be portrayed as a princess who warrants our
attention because an ambitious man has chosen her as his mate.
Because Campbell's complicated life and career defy traditional
mythmaking, her story is of exceptional interest and, perhaps, of
unusual importance. Her ascent to power may well mark the beginning of a shift in the Canadian perception of who can determine public policy and represent our national character.

In addition to bringing a novel presence to the drama of Canadian public life, Kim Campbell approaches politics with abilities and motives that differ from those of the men who have governed this country for most of the past 25 years. Although she presents herself as an intellectual, ideas are not as significant to her as they were to Pierre Elliott Trudeau, who had a clear and articulated vision of the nation he wanted to shape. Beyond being a fiscal conservative, Campbell has yet to show commitment to any tangible ideological principles. For her, "politics is the art of the possible."

Kim Campbell has strengths that will serve her well in the office of prime minister: she is an extremely hard worker who enjoys applying her fine mind to the business of government; her opinions on policy are usually formed in extensive discussions with experienced bureaucrats and skilled practitioners in the private sector; and she has shown a willingness to compromise, favoring middle-of-the-road solutions that ignite the least reaction. One of her greatest assets is a capacity to learn from her mistakes.

However, she does not possess the interpersonal skills that Brian Mulroney used so effectively to unite a once fractious caucus. The Conservative party is made up of urban and rural MPs, right-wing and Red Tories—all pushing their own agenda. It requires someone with remarkable diplomacy and charm to make this group sing out of the same hymnal. If she is to succeed in maintaining caucus solidarity, Campbell will have to learn to temper her arrogance and listen to other opinions even when she is convinced that she knows best.

Campbell can be expected to understand the alienation people feel in regions outside central Canada because she was born and bred on the West Coast. A vocal advocate of the Meech Lake and Charlottetown accords, Campbell is not likely to support a strong central government. Although this tendency may bode well for her in Quebec, where nationalist forces wield a great deal of influence, it may be her undoing in English Canada, which still prefers Trudeau's brand of federalism.

Like all of us, Campbell is not perfect; she can be quite dismissive of those who do not share her view of the world. On the other hand, she is dedicated, witty and vibrant. Canadians might be proud to have this clever, vital and intelligent woman as their head of state.

As Canada's first female prime minister, Campbell will be asked to make a difference to the lives of Canadian women. Her record on women's rights is mixed. Although she compromised her pro-choice views on abortion, she introduced a rape law that enshrines "no means no" as a principle of justice. As prime minister, she is likely to continue balancing feminism with more traditional views of women.

Kim Campbell's elevation to the office of prime minister shows that gender roles are changing. Her prominence proves to Canadian women that there is life beyond divorce—life that can be filled with prestige, responsibility and important work. The Conservative party and Canadian men can take pride in knowing that they are secure enough to accept female leadership, at least for a while.

1

A HOUSE DIVIDED

All happy families are alike but an unhappy family
is unhappy after its own fashion.

—*Tolstoy*

Elizabeth Gardiner Cook's eyes lit up with pride when she held her grandchild Avril Phaedra Douglas Campbell in her arms for the first time on March 10, 1947. Although baby Avril had been coaxed into the world a bit early, the induced delivery had gone well. She weighed in at a healthy seven pounds seven ounces and was a fine sight to behold with her reddish blond tufts of hair, her soft pink skin and blue eyes. Elizabeth had little regard for Avril's father, George, but she had every expectation that this new baby would inherit the robust individuality and joy of life that characterized the Cook and Gardiner clans. Their history was typical of so many English and Scottish immigrants who settled in British Columbia at the turn of the century.

Avril was the spitting image of Elizabeth's Ulsterman father, Jeremiah Augustus Hill Gardiner. Years earlier, when Jeremiah donned his Sunday best and asked for the hand of pretty Grace Graham of Glasgow, his prospective Scottish father-in-law raised a fuss. "There will be no mongrels in this family," he roared. Grace married the Irishman anyway. Tragically, Jeremiah was killed in a train accident in Glasgow at age 28, leaving his wife with three young children. Grace eventually married Andrew Bromley from the nearby town of Wishal, and sought a life with her new husband in Canada, far from the hardships of Scotland. When the family arrived at Nanaimo, on the east coast of Vancouver Island, in June 1911, the place was a magnet for ambitious pioneers, a bustling city prospering from a coal-mining boom and thriving on its rich farmland, abundant fishing and expanding lumber industry.

Petite but strong-willed, with flaming red hair and huge dark eyes, Grace's daughter Elizabeth caused quite a sensation. Fifteen-year-old Carl Cook marched home to tell his mother about the new lassie from across the sea. "I met the girl I'm going to marry," he announced. Although Carl had never travelled very far from Nanaimo, he too came from a family of pioneers. His ancestors were Baptists from Beverly, Massachusetts, part of the original wave of United Empire Loyalists who fled to Canada with their meagre possessions in 1783 at the end of the American Revolution. For a time, they put down roots in Bible Hill, now Truro, Nova Scotia. Soon, rumors of union between the colonies of Upper and Lower Canada aroused fears that they would be caught in another bloody civil war—this time between English- and French-speaking settlers. In 1870 they set out for Vancouver Island, a place reputed to be a paradise.

A family of sailors, the Cooks may have sailed around Cape Horn or travelled by railway and overland to Victoria, where they settled for a time. When land was offered to settlers around Nanaimo Lake, the Cooks jumped at the opportunity. They packed their belongings again and trekked 68 miles north along the narrow coastal road to the port city.

Carl's father, Ezra Stevens Cook, was a surveyor who had no trouble finding work in the area. The island's enormous century-old Douglas firs were being harvested, and there was a need for skilled men to plot the logging roads. Work was also being done on extending the Esquimalt and Nanaimo Railway to Port Alberni and Courtenay; and the increasing popularity of the horseless carriage made it necessary to widen and upgrade the road from Victoria to Nanaimo. With so much demand for his services, Ezra could easily afford the fine house he bought for his family on upscale Wallace Street. The six-bedroom Nova Scotia-style home boasted a wide veranda and property large enough for a vegetable garden, an orchard and a pasture for a cow.

Carl was studious and determined to have a career free from the backbreaking work of the English and Scottish laborers who immigrated to cut the redwoods, mine the coal fields and sail the fishing boats in pursuit of salmon, cod and herring. After completing high school, he left for Oregon, where he studied for a college degree in dentistry. During World War I, he interrupted his schooling to join the army but did not see action overseas.

When Carl graduated in 1920, he married Elizabeth, who had now begun her own profession as a schoolteacher. After working for two years in New Westminster with some other dentists, he earned enough money to start his own practice. He decided to settle in Port Alberni, a frontier town founded by the Hudson's Bay Company in 1856. With its dusty roads, rough-talking loggers and lack of electricity, the town was a far cry from civilized Nanaimo. However, it did have one saving grace: until Carl arrived, Port Alberni had no dentist.

Carl and Elizabeth's new home was the gateway to the west coast of the island. The town sat at the head of a natural deep sea waterway, nearly 30 miles from the Pacific Ocean. As the number of immigrants swelled, Port Alberni began to enjoy boom times. Sawmills soon flourished along the Somass River and so did commercial salmon fishing. Carl's practice grew along with his family. By the early 1930s, he and Elizabeth had three children—Shirley, Phyllis and Douglas. Two years separated the girls, while Douglas, the baby of the family, was six years younger than Phyllis. A third sister died at the age of three, before Douglas was born.

All three Cook children remember their childhood years as an active, happy time. Although Elizabeth could be stern, Carl was always easygoing. He loved to sing, dance and play the guitar. Phyllis says that her dad "could pick up any string instrument and play. He was a great deal of fun at bonfires and picnics. He loved kids."

Phyllis was exceptionally beautiful. Barely five feet tall, she had auburn hair, apricot skin and huge, dark brown eyes like her mother. "She was a real knockout," says Shirley, who remembers feeling competitive with her intelligent and attractive younger sister. "Phyllis was brilliant," she recalls. "One time our high-school principal said to my father, that in all the years, he had never had anyone with remotely as high an I.Q. as Phyllis." Not liking the way her friends referred to his clever, feminine daughter as "Phil," Carl began calling her Lissa, a name she would eventually adopt.

One summer day in 1939, Carl, an athlete and a sportsman, took the United Church Youth Group for a day of hiking on Mt. Arrowsmith, a 5,900-foot mountain east of Port Alberni. Shirley was part of the group, and Lissa desperately wanted to join the fun. "I'm going to come," she told her dad. "No, not today," he replied. Those were the last words she would hear him speak. On the way up the mountain, Carl stopped to tie his shoelace. Running to catch up with the kids, he suddenly dropped dead of a heart attack. He was 42.

When Carl died, Shirley was 16, Lissa 14 and Douglas 8. The loss of their fun-loving father was heart-wrenching for the children. In addition to the emotional pain, the family experienced financial hardship even though Carl had left Elizabeth enough money in investments to enable her to keep the children fed and clothed without her having to return to the classroom. The war in Europe also affected their lives. When Nazi armies invaded Poland in early September 1939, Canada entered the war, and Lissa was determined to join the war effort. Shirley recalls that "as soon as it started Phyllis said, 'They are going to have women in this war and I'm going to be in it.'" She promptly began studying Morse code, knowing the navy or army would have a use for recruits with this special skill.

In May 1943, at the age of 18, Lissa enlisted in the Women's Royal Canadian Naval Service. This branch of the Canadian Navy, known as the Wrens, was formed in July 1942 on the model of the British Women's Royal Naval Service. When the navy decided it could do with some help, Canadian women were asked to join up to perform on-shore jobs as stenographers, postal clerks, stewards, coders, cooks, transport drivers and teletype operators. Some recruits would learn to operate special wireless and loran shore stations to keep operational plots of the war at sea. Others with training as visual signallers would run base signal towers. Lissa found the prospect of doing such challenging work very appealing.

She started her life as a Wren earning 90 cents a day during three weeks of basic training at a naval establishment two miles outside Galt, Ontario. The "ship" was actually a group of brick buildings, commissioned as HMCS *Conestoga*, situated many miles from sea on 22 acres of land. Formerly known as the Grandview School for Girls, a correctional institution (and today the site of an abuse scandal), the Wrens' training centre still had bars on its windows.

Probationary Wrens were put through a strenuous program involving physical training, drills, discipline and navy protocol. They attended lectures and studied for tests on naval law and traditions, as well as doing everything required to maintain the centre and its three-acre vegetable garden. When Lissa completed her training at Galt, her pay was raised to 95 cents a day.

She took further training in Ottawa, St-Hyacinthe and Halifax, where she learned to operate HFDF, a high-frequency radar system that could track Nazi attack submarines patrolling off the east coast of Canada. Life as a Wren suited Lissa very well. "I loved it," she says. "It is very thrilling when you are 18 or 19 years old to really feel you are doing something to save lives like we did."

Before she left home for Galt, Lissa had caught the eye of Sgt. George Campbell, who worked in dentistry services at the army and naval camp recently built to defend Vancouver Island from an anticipated Japanese onslaught. Shirley had married John McPhail, an officer whose wealthy father promoted Algoma Steel and Great Lakes Power in Sault Ste. Marie, Ontario. One day John and George "were walking back to camp and George had seen my sister and was raving about this beautiful woman," remembers Shirley. But Lissa had many suitors and George did not impress her. "He asked me to marry him," says Lissa, "and I said, 'No, I'm going into the navy.'"

George could be extremely charming. He loved to fly kites, sing English barroom songs and play the ukulele. A master at mimicking accents, he delighted townsfolk with his stand-up comedy routines. "He'd have you lying in the aisles," remembers Lissa's brother, Doug. "He was generally a very entertaining fella." But the charm hid a troubled childhood.

Born in 1920 in Montreal, George was one of the three sons of Emma and George T. Campbell. Before World War I, George T.'s parents had emigrated from Glasgow to Montreal, where his father found work as a master baker. George T. was in the merchant marine and a stern disciplinarian of his three boys. "I was brought up to be seen and not heard," George recalls. "Coupled with that is do what you're told when you're told. I got some lickings when I was a kid—didn't leave any lasting bruises and [I] don't think it ever did me any harm, but it was a way of exercising discipline."

Emma came from the Orkneys and worked as a secretary, for a time handling the affairs of Saidye Bronfman, wife of liquor baron, Sam. Although George will not discuss his early days, it is known that his childhood was difficult. He says his father died when he was age two, but Lissa claims George T. ran off when the children were young, leaving the family penniless. Whatever the case, Emma struggled for a time until she met a man who promised to marry her if she got rid of the children. She handed nine-year-old George over to a Roman Catholic bachelor who took the boy first to Saskatchewan and later to Vancouver in 1936. "He had a lousy childhood," says one acquaintance. To this day, George has no contact with his only surviving brother, Carl, who lives in Montreal. "I am not even sure of the address any more," he says. "People don't keep in touch. Some people do and some people don't, I guess."

For a time George was placed in a Catholic boarding school until the war broke out. His dream of becoming a doctor evaporated when his stepfather enlisted and informed him he was on his own. "He was going to go to university," says one of the family, "but he didn't have any money to go back to school. He had to support himself, so he enlisted." In mid-1939, during the "phoney war," George joined the Coast Artillery, serving at several bases in the west until he was posted to Port Alberni. "I messed around in the army for a while [though] I had always wanted to get to the Seaforth Highlanders," he told E. Kaye Fulton of *Maclean's* magazine. Initially he was rejected because of poor eyesight. "I wear glasses, and for an infantry soldier, glasses were not considered to be too good," he explained.

Smitten with Lissa, the 23-year-old army sergeant kept track of her every posting. His letters and telegrams followed her to each new assignment. Although she loved the life of a Wren, the small-town girl frequently felt lonely. No sooner would she make some girl-friends and meet some boys than she would be transferred to another base. Consequently, even though she was not initially attracted to George, in 1944, when he moved from Camrose, Alberta, to Truro, Nova Scotia, near her posting in Moncton, she agreed to see him.

Lissa did the most important, absorbing work in her career as a Wren during the time she was posted in Moncton at the Coverdale military base. Her skills with radar were put to use tracking German submarines travelling in "wolf packs" as they hunted down convoy ships bound for the European warfront. "We were very close to the war," she says. "We knew darn well that most of those boys [in merchant convoys] would die . . . and we shed tears for all those sailors."

The constant barrage of letters, the loneliness and her proximity to George in Truro finally started to win Lissa over. However, the two married more out of necessity than growing love. "Unfortunately, in those days babies came when they wanted despite all your clever intentions," says Lissa. When Lissa became pregnant, she had to leave the Wrens. "It broke her heart," Shirley remembers. Soon after their 1944 wedding, Lissa made George change his name to Paul because she thought it sounded more interesting (though today he is again known as George).

Paul's persistence paid off. He had a life with the woman he loved. The couple were not married for long when he got something else that he wanted very much: an overseas posting. On October 28, 1944, he gave up his sergeant's stripes and joined the Seaforth Highlanders to help fight the war in Europe. He was sent first to England and then to Italy. "I sailed down to Italy and joined the regiment," he says.

In December the Seaforths joined the Allied pincer assault on the Italian city of Bagnacavallo, between the Lamone and Senio rivers. The Canadians advanced on the city, fighting house to house, as they dodged artillery fire and sturdy German "Tiger" tanks in the muddy fields. A major battle took place on December 16, and over the course of the next four days the Germans retreated in bloody ground fighting. Campbell was hit in the side with shrapnel on the seventeenth and was transferred to England to recuperate. "I got shrapnel. An explosion blew into what they call the loin. Various things were perforated," he recalls.

By May 1945 he was back in Vancouver at Shaughnessy Hospital, two months after Lissa had given birth to their first child. Although Lissa had endured a worrisome, difficult pregnancy because of a kidney infection, blond, blue-eyed Alix Paula Bernadette was a lovely, healthy baby.

During the first summer of Alix's life, the young family lived in a camp on Mt. Arrowsmith where Paul worked as a forestry lookout. They then moved to Victoria, where he could use his veteran's allowance to obtain a general arts degree at Victoria College. Over the next two years, Lissa spent a good deal of time with Alix and her mother in Port Alberni while Paul stayed in the city. In addition to going to college, he was also in and out of the hospital, suffering from abcesses of the shrapnel wound.

When Lissa became pregnant again, she chose to await the birth of her second child in Port Alberni, where she would have help caring for two-year-old Alix during her stay in hospital. (In those days, women were routinely kept in hospital for ten days after giving birth.) It was another difficult pregnancy for Lissa, who had lost more than ten pounds in her sixth month. The doctor decided to induce birth about three weeks earlier than the April arrival date.

Many people have asked Phyllis to explain the unusual names she chose for her baby: Avril Phaedra Douglas. Douglas, the name of her younger brother, and Avril, French for her daughter's anticipated month of birth, are easily understood. But Phaedra arouses much curiosity. The Greek name refers to an unlucky queen in ancient myth. Phaedra was the wife of King Theseus of Athens, who fell in love with her husband's illegitimate son, Hippolytus. She sent the handsome youth a note admitting her passion and declaring that all the women of her family seemed fated to be betrayed in love. When Hippolytus rejected her advances, Phaedra hanged herself from a lintel in the palace, forever afterwards giving her name connotations of tragedy.

Lissa's explanation of her choice of name is a simple one: she liked the way it sounded. She came across the name in a biography of Sarah Bernhardt, who had rave reviews on the Paris stage in a production of Racine's play based on the myth. "I had this funny idea she would be a public person and I thought maybe she would be an author and she could be called Avril Phaedra Douglas."

George has little idea what the names mean. "I've got to be honest with you, I wasn't thinking of anything," he says. "Avril was French for April, let's put it that way. Phaedra, I just read the other day, was a Greek goddess who suffered an untimely end. I didn't know any of that at the time other than it was a Greek goddess or princess or something."

Three months after Avril was born, Lissa and the girls left Port Alberni to live with Paul in Little Mount Camp, the veterans' barracks at Queen Elizabeth Park on the grounds of the University of British Columbia, where he was completing his B.A. The rent was cheap at $27 a month, but the quarters were cramped and uncomfortable. Money was tight and life seemed hard to Lissa. Living on a monthly allowance of $92, she remembers having to go shopping with only 20 cents in her purse. Nevertheless, their circumstances were not much different from those of other families who seemed happy enough living in the barracks. The Campbells' situation probably seemed especially difficult to Lissa because she and Paul were growing further apart.

One night when the baby was about a year old, Lissa woke to muffled sounds of choking coming through the thin wall separating her bedroom from the children's. When she hurried in to check on the girls, she saw that Avril's face was blue. She quickly opened the baby's mouth to see if there was anything lodged in her throat. Finding nothing, a panic-stricken Lissa rushed outside to a pay phone to call the doctor. After examining Avril, the doctor concluded she had bulbar polio, the most deadly form of the disease because it paralyzed the respiratory tract. "Let's get her out of here," he said, carrying the now blackish colored child into the ambulance.

Much to Paul and Lissa's relief, Avril did not have polio. However, she was seriously ill with septic laryngitis. The surgeon performed a tracheotomy, cutting into her windpipe to insert a tube so she could breathe. For ten days, the doctors refused to allow the parents to come anywhere near Avril, and Paul and Lissa could only look at their daughter through a one-way glass. "They said if she saw me she could cry and she could die if she cried," says Lissa. When Lissa and Elizabeth went to the hospital to take Avril home, the little girl cuddled in her grandmother's arms. "She wouldn't have anything to do with Phyllis at all," remembers her aunt Shirley. "Mother always felt that Kimmie turned against her [Lissa] then and she never got a chance to come back. That was an awful period."

It is tempting to read a great deal into this incident. There can be no doubt that Avril, sick, in pain and deserted by both parents, felt terrorized in the hospital. Such an early traumatic experience might have laid the psychological grounding for a fiercely independent personality. And Nana Cook might well have been right to think that the later estrangement between Avril and Lissa had been foreshadowed by their early separation.

Nevertheless, Lissa cared deeply about building a strong relationship with both girls. She was an affectionate, loving parent who enjoyed spending time with her children. She was fond of reading bedtime stories and would often take out her old books of

children's verse from the Port Alberni schoolhouse and recite po-
etry. "Forty Singing Seamen" and "The Highwayman" were two
favorites. Alix and Avril would sit wide-eyed as Lissa played the
piano and encouraged them to sing. "They liked to make little
concerts and sing and dance," their mother remembers.

Lissa recalls that each girl had her own talents. Alix learned to
read by the age of two and, in general, was more skilled academi-
cally than her sister. But Avril excelled at music, particularly the
piano. "When she was four she could play anything she heard on
the radio, like commercial songs. She'd just go over and play it."
The children's relationship with one another was characterized
by the usual sibling rivalries. Alix had her friends and interests, as
did Avril. "They went with a different crowd, so they weren't
close friends, but they were never enemies," says Lissa.

Not long after Avril's illness and just before his graduation
from UBC, Paul put a down payment on a small house in Burnaby,
a municipality adjoining Vancouver. Avril was very happy there.
She and Alix would climb Burnaby Mountain to pick berries and
play in a large field nearby. "My sister and I were great tomboys,"
she recently told writer Peter C. Newman. "We wore jeans and
shirts all the time and climbed trees and were quite wild. It was
just wonderful."

Because his marks were not good enough to qualify him for
medical school, Paul decided to become a lawyer. "I wanted to be
a doctor but I just couldn't get into medical school," he recalls.
"The demands were so heavy. My marks were fair but I guess I just
couldn't compete." He enrolled at UBC's law school and graduated
in 1953.

While Paul was studying, Lissa went to work to help support the
family. She taught herself to type and found a job as a secretary in
downtown Vancouver, on Hornby Street. After that she worked as
a receptionist in a doctor's office and, later, as a salesclerk in an art
shop. "The most I earned was $45 a week and he ended up a

lawyer and I ended up with no skills to earn a decent living that would have enabled me to look after the girls," she says.

When Paul started his own practice soon after receiving his degree, he moved the family into a comfortable white stucco house at 2707 West 33rd Avenue, near the corner of Trafalgar Street in the well-to-do middle-class district of Kerrisdale. The girls attended Kerrisdale Elementary School, a pleasant ten-minute walk from their home along tree-lined streets. The school offered students a challenging curriculum and a safe environment in which to grow.

There were Christmas concerts, an annual Fathers' Night, and a Family Fun Fair at which parents played games with the children and ate lunches they had packed. In May on Sports Day, the biggest event of the school year, Alix and Avril would join the other children in wearing elaborate costumes and decorating their bicycles for the parade. Both girls were excellent students, and Avril's favorite subject was English. About the only subject she did not like was gym, although Lissa says that she enjoyed watching track meets and basketball games.

Alix and Avril took dancing and piano lessons. Although Alix did not have as good an ear as her younger sister, she got more praise from their piano teacher. Lissa remembers being asked by Avril to play classical music assignments over and over again as she sat beside her on the piano stool. "I was being fooled, you see," says Lissa. "The teacher phoned me and said she's not even looking at the music. She is playing it by ear."

Avril was an avid reader. She had varied tastes, unlike Alix, who preferred Nancy Drew. From time to time, Avril was caught reaching for risqué books that her parents had placed on the top bookshelves.

Always self-confident and outgoing, Avril was eight when the local television station chose her for a small part on a children's program. Soon she was performing alongside such celebrities as

Little Richard. However, starring on TV caused problems for her with the other children at school. One day the teacher called Lissa to ask her daughter to stop bragging. "I explained [to Avril] what the counsellor said. And she said, 'Oh, I didn't know that.' The next day she came home, not shattered, and said 'I didn't do it once, Mom.' For a week she would say 'I didn't do it once.'"

In grade seven, Avril entered Point Grey Junior High where she was the star of that year's concert. She wrote, produced and directed a show featuring a Roaring Twenties dance group. With her best friend, April Marshall (née Wheeler), she sewed the frills on their skirts and giggled as they practised the Charleston to the record her dad had bought her. "I can remember standing and looking down at this line of dancers kicking their legs and coming onto the patio," recalls George. The show was so success-ful that the girls were asked to perform at an outdoor event for youngsters in the park near the family home.

Religion fascinated Avril. For a few years, Lissa took the girls to the United Church where they sang in the choir. But Avril soon lost interest in the bland services of that denomination after a friend invited her to attend the local Pentecostal Church. She was moved by the power of the gospel music, remembers Lissa. "She came home singing those songs and she said, 'Could I change and go to the Pentecostal Church?'" April Marshall also recalls that Avril was very interested in religious questions and that she wanted to visit the synagogue as well as all the local churches.

"She had this great sense of justice," says her friend, recollect-ing a time when she went on a vacation with the Campbells to Shuswap. One day, she and Avril went over to flirt with some boys who were playing near logs on the beach. A boy grabbed Marshall's wrist and snatched away her sterling silver bracelet, a gift from her mother. "I was really mad," she remembers. She chased the boy to the pier and the bracelet slipped out of his hands into the water. "I was starting to take off my shoes and dive in when Avril said, 'No. He has to get it.' She browbeat the guy to keep diving until he found it."

Despite all their outward talents, successes, interests and friendships, Alix and Avril grew up in a home that was seriously troubled because their parents were miserable together. Lissa says that soon after her wedding she realized that she had made a "colossal mistake" in marrying Paul. He was hot-tempered and too caught up in his own world to have much time for his wife and young daughters. According to his wife, he called household chores "squaw work" and refused to help.

Shirley remembers one particular incident that illustrates Paul's irrational treatment of Lissa. Upon coming home after winning one of his first big cases, Paul declared, "I won. I won." When Lissa replied, "Oh, I knew you would do it, dear," he flew into a rage. "He went almost hysterical," says Shirley. "He said, 'Everybody else thinks I'm so wonderful. Everybody else thinks I did something nobody else could do. Only my wife would say, 'Oh, I knew you would do it.'"

The relationship deteriorated further when Paul's mother, Emma, arrived unannounced at their home not long after her son graduated from law school. "I've come to spend the rest of my life here," she said, much to Lissa's horror. Although Emma stayed with the young family only for a brief period before she found herself an apartment, Lissa continued to resent her mother-in-law's demands on her husband's time. Paul also began to spend more and more weekends away from the family with his new motorboat. Lissa suspected that he was seeing other women.

The marriage became unbearable in 1957 when a freak accident almost crippled Lissa for life. Balmy Vancouver had experienced one of its rare snowfalls, and Lissa decided to have some winter fun with her children. She cheerfully bundled up the girls, grabbed the toboggan and trudged off to the steep hill on the golf course. While Alix and Avril played in the new snow, Lissa jumped on the toboggan for a solo slide. As she flew down the hill, she suddenly hit a patch of ice. She was tossed high into the air and landed hard on the ice. The bone in her left hip shattered into fragments.

Today, Lissa does not feel that she got adequate treatment after her accident. Although doctors operated promptly and inserted a stainless steel plate into her hip, no one bothered to tell her to take calcium to strengthen the bone. When she later developed osteoporosis, the injury became much worse.

At the age of 33, Lissa became an invalid. She remembers that she could barely walk when she returned home from the hospital. The pain was horrible and made it difficult for her to get out of bed. Fortunately, Alix and Avril were wonderful helpers. In the mornings they slipped on her socks, slid a dress over her shoulders and fetched her crutches. Paul consented to hire a housekeeper, although he was otherwise unsympathetic to his wife's plight. "Her husband didn't take into account that she was suffering terrible pain from the prosthesis," says Lissa's brother, Doug, a retired army technician. "Things would come loose and grind away inside the bone. He was not the least bit sensitive about it."

Over the next two years, doctors performed three other operations, including a bone graft on the damaged hip. The pain was severe, but at least Lissa was able to walk with a cane and continue working at the art shop. A big disappointment after the accident was being unable to dance to the music of her favorite bands. She remembers that Paul called her a "cripple" and teased her about the women he claimed to be seeing: "He would come home and describe it all in detail." She says he even began to push her around. She never discussed their problems with Alix and Avril, but there was one three-week period when she had to stay home from work.

Campbell will not discuss Lissa's allegations, but he denies them emphatically. "That can leave the impression in the eye of the beholder that the reason Mr. Campbell doesn't want to talk about it is because he's guilty, which, of course, is not the case at all," he said, referring to himself in the third person, when questioned about Lissa's accusations in May 1993 by Stephen Brunt of *The Globe and Mail*. "Whatever she says, I don't intend to get into a dialogue about it because it won't serve any purpose for Kim. You'll just have to believe what you want to believe."

Lissa says she asked Paul for a divorce, but he refused. In those days the divorce laws favored the wage earner unless it could be proved that the husband was committing adultery. Determined to escape her marriage, she hired an ex-Mountie to follow her husband and get some evidence that she could use to sue for divorce. But the detective was never able to take photographs of Paul in a compromising situation.

On a bright Saturday afternoon in 1958, Lissa limped into a local grocery store. Working behind the counter was a handsome, athletic man whom she had spotted from time to time on Sundays at church. Bill Vroom, the son of a wealthy Dutch building contractor, was lending a hand to his friend who owned the store. Lissa and Bill struck up a conversation. "Come and have a cup of coffee with me," he said. Over coffee Bill told her that he was a salesman for a company called Northwestern Supplies. Lissa also learned that he was unhappily married with three young children and that he felt as trapped and sad as she did. He had tried to leave his wife three times, once going as far away as Alaska. Before too long Lissa and Bill were meeting regularly to share the miseries of their lives over coffee and cigarettes. "He was just darn nice and we had a lot fun," she says. "He had no conscious charm, he was just plain genuine."

After many clandestine encounters at coffee shops and a frequent exchange of flirtatious glances at Ryerson United Church, Lissa and Bill fell in love. Neither Paul nor Bill's wife, Joyce, suspected anything about the affair. Eventually, Bill asked Lissa to run off with him to the French Riviera. She recalls that Bill said: "I can't stand it any more. I've got to go. Will you come?" They could sail, forget their troubles and lead lives filled with love and romance.

Lissa was attracted to Bill's vitality and thirst for adventure. Living on the West Coast, he had developed a love of the sea and a passion for sailing. Even though he had a heart condition, he did not allow his ailment to limit him. For example, after he was discharged from the army in 1939 because of his bad heart, he signed on with the merchant marine in the Pacific. A few years later, in 1942, determined to take part in the war against the Axis powers, he tried to enlist in the United States Navy. He arrived in Pearl Harbor from New Guinea and rushed over to the U.S. naval recruitment centre to join up the day after Japanese bombers sank most of America's ships. When the Americans turned him away because he was not a U.S. citizen, he decided to give the Canadian forces one more try. This time the Royal Canadian Navy was delighted to have someone with Bill's merchant marine experience, regardless of the bad heart. Although he would not see action on the high seas, he was put to work as an instructor training newly recruited sailors. While teaching in the navy, he obtained his international navigation papers and could sail anywhere in the world.

In the summer of 1959, Lissa resolved to give up living the sham of the perfect marriage in the upscale neighborhood. "I just realized I couldn't hold out any longer," she says. "I just had to go." Shirley recalls that one doctor had told Lissa she had a bone disease that would claim her life within a year. She thinks that this dire prediction influenced her sister's decision to run off with Bill and spend what remained of her life in sunny climes.

Before she could leave, Lissa felt that she had to do something with Alix and Avril, as she did not want them to stay with her husband. Arguing that her hip injury made it impossible for her to take care of both the children and the house, she pleaded with

Paul to send the two girls, then aged 14 and 12, to boarding school for a year. Reluctantly, he agreed. However, her plan almost went awry when she discovered that all the boarding schools in Vancouver were filled up.

Since the local Catholic institutions would accept only children who had been raised in the faith, Lissa was in despair—until she remembered that a cousin from Seattle had gone to St. Ann's Academy in Victoria. Lissa called the convent school and was delighted to discover that there was room for both girls. The nuns did not mind Alix and Avril's Protestant upbringing as long as the girls understood that they would be required to study catechism and take communion with the rest of the school.

In September, Lissa and Paul bundled off their daughters to Victoria to be taught and cared for by the sisters of St. Ann. The tension and violence in their parents' marriage must have been a great strain on the girls, and it is no surprise that Avril did not seem to be disappointed at the prospect of being torn away from her friends and plunked down in a convent known for its strict rules and discipline. "She told me she wanted to go," remembers April Marshall. "She wasn't in tears or anything like that. As far as I recall it was like an adventure."

Soon after Lissa's children had been sent away, Bill went to the train station and purchased two one-way tickets on *The Canadian* to Montreal. He then arranged passage aboard the *Ibernia* to London. All was going smoothly for the lovers until the moment Lissa was leaving the house to meet Bill. On the morning of the fine October day on which they planned to elope, just as she was carrying the last suitcase to the car she had packed with her belongings, Paul arrived home unexpectedly. "He was supposed to be at work," she recalls. "So I dropped the suitcase behind a bush and walked over to see him. I said, 'What's the matter?' and he said 'I have a corn on my foot and it's killing me so I've made an appointment this afternoon with the podiatrist.' I walked into the house with him so he wouldn't look behind and see the car loaded to the devil with suitcases." When Paul had settled into his study, Lissa picked up her coat and shouted goodbye. "And that was it," she says. "I vanished from sight." She left the car at the station with a note identifying it as belonging to Paul. Later she would regret that she didn't sell it.

Deeply in love and relieved to be free of their unhappy marriages, Bill and Lissa enjoyed themselves in London. Still, Lissa felt enormously guilty about abandoning her daughters and wrote to Paul to say she might return home. But soon she decided against the idea and found work in a blood clinic while Bill, determined to live life to the fullest, bought a 42-foot cutter, built in 1900 by Luke, the English boat designer. The cutter was in tip-top shape, without a single soft board. He refitted the boat, named it the *Banshee*, and sailed off with Lissa and their little Siamese cat across the choppy waters of the Bay of Biscayne. They spent a year onboard their boat, sailing the Mediterranean by day and drinking fine wine over dinner in the evenings. Lissa's health began to improve. When their money ran out in Portugal, Bill sold the *Banshee* and moved them into a lovely apartment in Cannes.

Because he had his navigation papers, Bill found it easy to hire himself out as a captain on the yachts of millionaires. Lissa went along as part of the crew, usually working as a cook. It was a romantic and adventurous life, far away from the suburban routine of their previous existence. As they sailed together on far-off seas, their children were growing up without them.

It would be ten years before Avril Campbell would see her mother again.

2

COMING OF AGE

You looked at Kim and you could pretty well
forecast she was going to be successful.

—*Darlene Currie,*
Campbell's physical education teacher

St. Ann's Academy in Victoria was an impressive four-storey
grey brick building with a grand façade and an enormous curv-
ing staircase facing Humboldt Street at the edge of Beacon Hill
Park on the sea coast. In the front garden, to the side of the wide
laneway bordered by trees, there was a shrine dedicated to Mary,
where the crowning of the May Carnival Queen took place each
year. Another smaller shrine to the Virgin was located at the back
where the junior students ran and played. Mass was recited in
Latin in a well-proportioned chapel with a vaulted ceiling supported by two rows of partially fluted columns with Ionic capitals.
The altar was ornate, and 172 rosettes formed the motif on the
arches of the ceiling. The dark-panelled hallway led to a museum

and a library known as the Blue Room. In the carpeted parlor, decorated with the paintings of Sister Mary Osithe, there was a piano around which generations of students met to sing and talk.

From 1858 to 1973, the Sisters of St. Ann worked to educate girls in a peaceful, disciplined and ordered environment. Although St. Ann's has closed its doors and the building now stands vacant, when Alix and Avril arrived in 1959, the school was thriving. A new wing had been added to the secondary school the year before, and both day students and boarders, dressed in white blouses and blue tunics, filled the classrooms. It was a few years before Vatican II and the nuns still wore habits. The sisters could be strict with their students but were known as an order that cultivated compassion and feminine understanding. Free from the stress and turmoil that characterized their family life, Alix and Avril seemed content in the serene and comfortable atmosphere of the academy.

The girls had a month to settle in before the letter from Lissa arrived informing them that their world had been changed forever. Their mother had given the letter to a close friend to post on the day she boarded the train with Bill. Lissa wrote that she could not stay with Paul any longer. Although their mother's misery came as no surprise to them, neither Alix nor Avril had any idea that she had been seeing another man. Because the girls were not close to Paul, their mother had been the bedrock of their family and the emotional centre of their lives. Lissa would say later that she believed her children understood and sympathized with her flight from her disastrous marriage. "I think they understood," she says. "I don't say they liked it. I'm sure they didn't and I'm sure they missed me a lot."

Psychologists say that traumatic events in the history of families tend to be repeated from one generation to another. This maxim certainly seems to hold true for Lissa's departure from her husband and children. When she left, her eldest daughter, Alix, was 14—

the same age Lissa had been when death separated her from Carl, her beloved father. As for Paul, his wife's betrayal paralleled that of his mother, who had given him over to a stranger at the age of nine. With Lissa gone, Alix and Avril were required to grow up, like Paul, without a mother. Thus, by disappearing when she did, Lissa repeated a pattern of behavior on both sides of the family.

Avril was so shaken by the break-up that she dropped her given name and started to call herself Kim, the name of one of Uncle Doug's children. (At times, she used Avril Kim or A. Kim.) "I suppose my desire to change my name had something to do with the thought that my mother left and the kind of trauma that children go through under those kinds of circumstances," she explains. "It is the kind of thing that children often do when they are faced with a serious emotional trauma. I think that was why I did it and why I took the name."

Paul, who began calling himself George again when Lissa left, does not remember why his youngest daughter suddenly changed her name. All he recalls is that she dropped Phaedra for A. Kim. "I remember her coming home and telling me she had asked everybody to call her Kim and asked if I could. I had no problem with that. I never thought of any complications arising from it. Who knows, it might have taken me a week to get used to it. I don't remember ever having been corrected by her saying, 'Dad, call me Kim.' I think we picked it up right away."

Alix, while probably just as distraught as her sister, did nothing dramatic to mark her mother's flight. Perhaps, on some level, she accepted Lissa's action. Much later she commented, "Kim and I had known the marriage wasn't good for years."

Kim was not inclined to share her anguish with either the nuns or the other students. Sister Eileen Gallagher, Kim's eighth-grade teacher, says that she never once discussed her mother's departure or what led to it. However, Kim and Alix became closer than they ever had been. Far away from their old friends in Kerrisdale, the girls had to rely on each other for emotional support. Lissa says that her daughters became the "closest of friends" at St. Ann's. Kim also sought solace in a new religion. She became an Anglican—an act that, like her change of name, perhaps indicated a wish for a new identity.

In contrast to many children who would have displayed depression, anger or rebellion, Kim dealt with her feelings by throwing herself into her schoolwork and extracurricular activities with a zeal that could not be matched by the other students. She had the highest marks in her class of 30 students. Sister Gallagher recalls that Campbell was an outstanding citizen of the school. "I remember her very well as a perfect student whose I.Q. tests were beyond perfect scores. She was very courteous and would brighten any classroom. She had a spontaneous manifestation of a sense of justice toward native people as well as others even though she was only 12 years old." Determined to be crowned St. Ann's May Carnival Queen, an honor that involved raising money for the school, Kim won the contest hands down. "She had placards and everything," recalls Alix.

When the girls returned home for the summer, George announced that he would not pay for another year at St. Ann's. He asked Elizabeth to come and look after her granddaughters. "He told my mother to come and she foolishly did it," recalls Lissa, who kept in contact from Cannes through a frequent exchange of letters with her mother and daughters.

George explains why Alix and Kim did not return to St. Ann's in a different way. "The most interesting thing for me, which I remember," he says, "is that the girls wanted to come home from boarding school and look after Dad. And that's what they did. Beyond that, we never discussed the break-up at the time. As you can imagine, it was painful."

An outgoing, petite, attractive, dark-haired woman, only five years older than Alix, offered George comfort. Virginia Vessey, or

Ginny as the kids called her, met George in August 1960, two days after she had moved to Vancouver from her home town of Charlottetown. She became the second Mrs. Campbell in February 1962, when George's divorce became final. "Virginia was very difficult and wouldn't help Kimmie at all," recalls Shirley. "She didn't like having Kimmie in the house." Kim would get up early and flee the house to Prince of Wales Secondary School, a 25-minute walk from home. "It meant she had lots of time for study," adds Shirley.

Ginny, who amicably divorced George in 1969, insists that she got along well with Kim but not Alix. George's oldest daughter resented Ginny because of their closeness in age, while Kim was apparently happy to be in her company. "Kim used to introduce me as her mother and she used to call me 'Little Mother,' " says Ginny, who is remarried and lives in Bass Lake, California. "I encouraged her always to have her friends over to the house. She was allowed to have house parties and things like that." To this day, Ginny remains a close friend of George's and says the relationship ended because the two simply grew apart. Lissa's accusations against George are out of character with the man she married, says Ginny. "I find that awful hard to believe. He's a very gentle, kind man. I wasn't there, but I never saw him raise a hand against anybody."

Kim continued to excel in all facets of her life outside the home. One of the most popular students at school, she was also at the top of her class. She had no qualms about wearing a false beard and dressing in bizarre costumes to advertise school dances. At concerts, she strummed her guitar and sang "Puff, the Magic Dragon." "She was so friendly. She was so warm. She was so bubbly," recalls classmate Gina Steer. Even her closest friends did not know the private pain she suffered because she did not discuss Lissa's absence or the new woman in George's life with anyone but Alix. George says Kim never allowed people to see her vulnerability. "Kim will attempt to mask her hurt. One way she'll do that is that she won't cry. If she doesn't cry people might get the impression that it is not impacting on her when, in fact, it is. She is just restraining the tears."

Ralph White, Kim's popular six-foot, blond-haired boyfriend in grades nine and ten, recollects that there was "a bit of friction" between Kim and the extraverted Ginny. Yet he is certain that Alix and Kim somehow worked out their differences with their young stepmother. "They got to know her, and I remember going over and it was just like three sisters. It was kind of unusual, but then again, it was unusual for people to get divorced in those days." White was amazed at his high-school sweetheart's ability to put her troubles behind her. Despite the loss of her mother, she always presented herself as a "fun and bubbly person." He cannot remember ever talking seriously with Kim about Lissa. "She either buried it so deep that it didn't come out or maybe she got subconsciously involved in all these things at school to forget." The only time he recalls Kim's mentioning Lissa was when she gave him a bracelet engraved with the name "Ave", which she said had been a present from her mother.

In high school Kim was part of a group of active teenagers. On weekends they threw parties at each other's homes and danced to the records of Jerry Lee Lewis or Elvis (two of Kim's favorites) in rec rooms or at school dances. Sometimes they would go up to Whistler for picnics and swimming. In those innocent teenage times, there were no drugs and the use of alcohol was minimal. Kim would often entertain her friends on the family piano, where she would sing her own lyrics. Even though she was very comfortable with her regular circle, Kim was, according to April Marshall, "always looking to make new friendships, to find out what makes people tick and what they thought."

Those close to Kim remember that she always exuded self-confidence and that at times she expressed great ambition. "The rest of us were talking about becoming nurses and dating cute boys," says Steer. "She told me she wanted to be the prime minister of the country. I didn't know who the prime minister even was then. To me, that was like saying I'm going to be the Queen of England." George says his youngest daughter came home one day when she was 14 and announced she wanted to head the United Nations: "I think she felt the secretary general had to be the most important person in the world because that would be the person to guide the movement of the countries of the world getting along. She said she thought that would be a wonderful thing to be."

In grade 11, Kim's boyfriend was handsome, broad-shouldered Bob Jackson, described as a "magnetic personality" in the yearbook. At six foot four, the popular "Mr. Sos" was Prince of Wales's star athlete in basketball and rugby. Bob, now a real estate agent in Cleveland, Ohio, had just lost his father when he met Kim. Despite his popularity, he had little self-esteem. Kim took him under her wing: "She really helped me because she sort of raised me up beyond what I had been. She gave me an awful lot of self-confidence that I didn't have before I started dating her. I felt better about myself through our relationship."

For more than a year Bob spent virtually every day with Kim, usually in the recreation room of the Campbell home. He remembers her as someone who had her life planned out. She wanted to go to university and she was fascinated with learning more about people through deep conversations. But, even though Kim was always willing to explore Bob's feelings, she would rarely discuss her own troubles, particularly the loss of her mother. "The story eluded me. I wasn't sure what was going on," says Jackson. "I knew she missed her mother. She had this pride in her mother that came through in conversations." Jackson believes that Kim was buoyant and upbeat most of the time because she was masking "sad feelings."

Kim seemed to be the glue that held the family together, Jackson remembers. She was intensely proud of Alix and never seemed to have an unkind word to say about her father. "There was no anger or anything toward her father. In fact, there was a lot of respect for him. She talked about him with pride and the things he was doing—his accomplishments—maybe even to the point of aggrandizing them." At the time Jackson knew Kim, Alix was dating Bill Oakenfu, a laborer who George thought was beneath her. When Alix dropped out of school, Kim did not criticize her, even though she probably did not approve. "She was sort of defending why her sister wasn't doing anything by saying her sister was really smart and really clever," says Jackson. "She said a lot of kind things about her."

George did not seem to take a very active role in raising his two daughters. He spent most of his time either at the Vancouver courthouse, where he worked as a prosecutor, or on his speedboat. When he took up scuba diving, he devoted many weekends to exploring the depths of the ocean. "I guess in large measure they raised themselves," he says. "I was there if I was needed, but for the most part they got up and went to school." George seems to have had no clue what his daughters were doing apart from the fact that Kim was active in school politics: "I really didn't know that much about their life outside the house. There were always boys and girls around the house who used to come for parties. But other than that I didn't really know too much of what their interests were outside school." Unlike many parents, he was not concerned whether his children were experimenting with sex: "If it's the business of love or that sort of stuff, whatever they did I wasn't aware of it."

Kim's friends have fond memories of George. They liked the fact that he ignored them. After greeting them warmly at the door, he generally stayed out of the way. "There were no restrictions put on Kim and she was responsible enough to take care of her own independence," says Gina Steer. "The kids were free to bring their friends home," George explains. "The monitoring was modest." However, on at least one occasion, he used his authority as a city prosecutor to make an impression. In a bizarre incident,

George called the police when the girls were throwing a party in the rec room. A couple of older boys had smuggled some beer into the basement and George had no desire to remonstrate with them himself: "I picked up the phone and called the dispatcher and asked them to have a dog car come around. A few minutes later, the car drove up at the front and the driver got out. I happened to know who he was and he had his leash. He started to walk around the corner of the house and maybe somebody had seen him come out, but these guys went legging it out the side gate and down the road and that was the end of that."

In her final year of high school, Kim ran for president of the student council. It was quite a challenge for a girl to seek an office that had been a wholly male preserve. Her opponent was Fred Grauer, editor of the fine arts section of the student newspaper and a scion of the family that founded B.C. Electric. Fred, a member of the badminton and basketball teams, was as active as Kim in student affairs. Her campaign stressed the need for more school spirit and for students to raise money to support school activities. On her publicity poster, she asked, "What Can Kim Campbell Do For You?" and promised to "help increase school income through events such as sock hops" and by "organizing transportation to school games." Her campaign buttons had squares cut from Peanuts cartoons with a caption that declared: "Snoopy Needs Kim Campbell As President."

Kim won, capturing more than 50 percent of the vote from the student body of 1,100. The win was a testament to her popularity, although Grauer had inadvertently contributed to her victory by putting off many students with his razzle-dazzle campaign that included balloons. "Everybody thought Grauer was a bit much. He came on too strong," says Kim's grade-12 classmate Ronald Freeland. Kim was just 16 when she became the first female president in the school's 42-year history. "I thought it was time to try some new ideas and get a girl elected," she told the student newspaper. At only five foot four, Kim joked she had no fear of getting co-operation from the 15 other members of the council: "There are some pretty big boys on it, but I'll have a big gavel." Darlene Currie, who taught Kim physical education, remembers how everyone was so impressed that this tiny girl, described in the school paper as "a pretty strawberry blond," had won the presidency. "I came from a generation where girls ran to be secretary of the student council, and here she was running for the top. It was a real breakthrough," she recalls. "It provided a whole new avenue for kids in the school."

That same year, Campbell was on the team that Prince of Wales sent to appear on "Reach for the Top," the well-known TV game show. She also won the grade 12 girls' merit award and was valedictorian of her class. In the address she delivered at graduation ceremonies in 1964, Kim spoke about the close friendships made at Prince of Wales as well as the responsibilities of leadership: "For as life goes on in its perpetual cycles, each generation must be groomed to take the reins of responsibility." There was little doubt in the minds of her classmates that she would be successful. "She was really a unique person," says Steer. "She is the type of person that even if she wasn't destined to be prime minister you knew she was destined for great things. She was so self-assured."

In the fall of 1964, Kim arrived at the campus of the University of British Columbia, where, not surprisingly, she majored in political science. Determined to become the first female president of the freshman class, she conducted her campaign with the same zeal and good humor that had been so successful at Prince of Wales. When the new undergraduates gathered for the annual frosh retreat, Kim was in the forefront—cracking jokes, playing her guitar and chatting up students like a political pro. When she filed her nomination papers for the October 14 Frosh Society vote, she was confident that she could pull off a victory.

The 17-year-old freshman faced off against two men in a contest that was ground-breaking for those conservative times. Women on campuses all over North America were just beginning to tear down sexist barriers that relegated them to lesser roles on student councils. In her campaign at UBC, Kim stressed her superior qualifications while using an easy-going, tongue-in-cheek banter that was soothing and almost motherly. In an article in the *Ubyssey*, the student newspaper, she wrote: "Got a yen to have someone look out for you for a change? You're new at UBC, you're not really sure what's going on, and now some crazy female wants your vote for Frosh President." Pledging to make the Frosh Society more responsive, Kim promised to offer students "a wider variety of events and better advertising of events."

The election was a shoo-in for Kim who beat her closest rival, Gordon Murphy, by 100 votes on the second ballot. More than a quarter of the frosh cast their ballots—nearly double the turnout of the year before. "My aim is to unify frosh and give them an identity this year," she declared after the votes were counted. Nonetheless, a sampling of comments in the *Ubyssey* shows that her success elicited a mixed response from students who were unaccustomed to having a female leader. "She seems a lot more emphatic than the boys" and "it's an indication of things to come" were on the positive side. Negative views were blatantly sexist: "a girl can't handle a man's job" and "she bounces around a lot" typified the complaints.

Some men just could not stomach the thought of a woman heading a major student organization. Not long after the frosh election, student John Kelsey ridiculed the new president in the *Ubyssey*. "There's nothing more gratifying than several women in their servile places. Nothing more appalling than one who gets out of it," he wrote. "[A man] must beat them into submission, showing no quarter, allowing no favor. And when he has successfully subjugated one, he must start on another." In a skilful bit of repartee, Campbell demolished Kelsey: "Women have waited patiently for

the right time to assert themselves openly. Opposition such as em-
anates from the nit-wit above proves the time is now."

Conceding that men are superior to women in cooking, pushing a vacuum and washing dishes, Kim suggested that males stick
to that important business and allow women to "save the world
from the terrible mess that men have made of it." Women's time
has come, she claimed: "What's all this garbage about women trying to dominate the world? Women ought to and women do. The
old platitude about a woman behind every man is no joke. But
now is the time to stop letting men take credit for what we are
accomplishing. Rise, women, let's tidy up the world."

When classes ended in the summer, Kim was not permitted to
relax and have fun with her friends. She had to work to pay for
her education. "She recognized the work ethic," George says in
explaining his unwillingness to foot the bill for university. "You
don't get anything for nothing. Kim didn't expect to get anything
for nothing." Kim found work at a fish-packing plant in Prince
Rupert, where she earned more than she would have in many
other jobs. "It was hard and it was smelly and icy cold on their
hands," says her aunt Shirley. "Fish packers earned every nickel
they got." Wearing overalls and a bandana, Kim cleaned fish and
shoved the slippery fillets into boxes. Late that summer, she left
the plant determined never to work in a fish plant again. To this
day she cannot eat halibut.

While Kim was gutting and packing halibut, Alix was in
London for a first visit with Lissa since she had left the family six
years before. Bill was now running boats out of London and earning a good living at $300 a day. Kim told Lissa that she could not
come because she was "working too hard." Whatever her reasons,
Kim chose not to face her mother at that time, although they kept
in touch by mail. Kim wrote Lissa "long detailed letters" and sent
"little clippings" when she became president of Prince of Wales's
graduating class and first female president of the frosh class at UBC.

Returning to university in the fall, Kim was less involved politically, although her social life was as active as ever. One of her most enjoyable pursuits was participating in a small group that performed operettas by Gilbert and Sullivan. In the following year, Nathan Divinsky, a math professor who had just returned from a sabbatical in London, joined the group. Even though he did not fit anyone's idea of Prince Charming, Kim found the older intellectual immensely attractive. Twenty-two years her senior, he was unlike the tall, Adonis-like young athletes Kim had been dating. Divinsky was short and plump, with flaring eyebrows and hair as frizzy as Albert Einstein's.

A brilliant scholar and a master at chess, Divinsky was vital and exuberant, with a complex mind and a razor-sharp wit. He was a Russian Jew, a first-generation Canadian, whose family had settled in north Winnipeg. CBC journalist Larry Zolf remembers Divinsky, nicknamed "Tuzie," and Allan Gotlieb as his counsellors at a B'nai Brith camp in Manitoba: "The camp was made up of rich and poor kids, and I remember Tuzie used to beat Gotlieb in chess matches with his back to him. And I remember that Tuzie had an enormous ego."

Divinsky, who received his Ph.D. in mathematics from the University of Chicago in 1950, aspired to be a renaissance man. A gourmet, pianist and champion bridge player, he had written several books on mathematics and edited both *Canadian Chess Chat* and *The Good Food Guide to Vancouver*. Just before meeting Kim, he had attended the world chess olympics in Cuba, where Fidel Castro had presented him with an elaborate chess set. A devoted follower of Ayn Rand, he had political views resembling those of a nineteenth-century libertarian. He once wrote that "we should kiss the feet of developers" and "let's not look down our noses at greed and profit." Acquisitiveness has always appeared to be central to Divinsky's view of the world. According to him, "Most of the things that are created and done positively in our society are done by private enterprise. It's the profit motive."

Divinsky's opinions about women, particularly poor ones, could best be described as unenlightened. He once told the Progressive Conservative Club at UBC that single women who become pregnant should give up their babies and not expect the state to support them. "No one asked her to uncross her legs," he explained, while launching into an attack on unemployment insurance and welfare programs. "Kings never lived as good as people on welfare in Vancouver," he added, arguing that welfare is a problem created by women who seek to live off society. "Women who run away from their husbands, where the husband is the breadwinner of the family, should not get public assistance," he declared. "They should never have left their husbands in the first place." Such opinions were certainly at odds with Kim's expressed views of the role of women.

When Divinsky met Kim, he had three teenage daughters and a disintegrating marriage. Betty, his former wife, says that for years she begged him to grant her a divorce, but he refused. In 1966, upon returning from his sabbatical in London, he moved into an apartment at 1275 Pacific Avenue because Betty would not let him back into their house. When Tuzie was spotted wining and dining a pretty sophomore, Betty saw her chance to divorce him and get a decent settlement. She hired private detectives to follow him in order to see if they could collect evidence that would help her case. Divinsky finally agreed to grant Betty the divorce, which became final in 1967.

In 1990, Alix told *Chatelaine* magazine that Kim was attracted to Divinsky's mind and his interests in fine cuisine and classical music. "Nathan had a lot to teach her, and she was hungry to learn," she explained. "He taught her the aplomb she has today. He introduced her to very intellectual circles." Aunt Shirley understands Kim's interest in Tuzie a bit differently: "I think he attracted her because he was so kind and the father that she didn't have. Really, she could talk to him. He was a very nice fatherly type." A friend of Tuzie's concurs: "He was somebody you could comfortably rely on. He was a big joker and kibitzer and had all the fantasies of a father."

Kim grew in several ways through her relationship with Divinsky. He convinced her to see a psychiatrist to help her deal with her emotional difficulties. Sessions with her doctor allowed her to verbalize some of the private agony she had endured for so long. Tuzie's friends recall that she became more willing to discuss the problems in her family and to admit that she had felt very lonely in her adolescence.

Not long after meeting Tuzie, Kim moved into Hester Webber's boarding house at 1270 West 11th Avenue, near the campus. She says that she had become "somewhat estranged" from her father. According to Lissa and Shirley, Kim was angry at George for forc-ing her to put herself through university while he earned a big salary as a prosecutor. After one season at the fish plant, Kim spent her summer months either working on the mayonnaise line at the Kraft factory or clerking at the Bay to pay for her educa-tion. To this day, she flares up when journalists liken her to Pierre Trudeau, who was born to millions. "I didn't have any money. I was living on my own. I was not born with a silver spoon in my mouth," she told Peter C. Newman. "That's why, when people compare me to Pierre Trudeau, I think, 'Oh, God, you couldn't have two more different lives.'"

In her final year of university, Kim Campbell was drawn back to student politics, and she was elected a vice-president of the Alma Mater Society. Campbell jokingly told a reporter from the Ubyssey that she had won the student council spot because she was "cuddlier" than her male opponent. But others took a differ-ent view of student power. Radicalism was rising on campuses throughout North America and UBC was no exception. Students were protesting the Vietnam War and demanding a bigger say in running the university. Although Campbell did not join the protests, she agreed that students ought to have a greater role in university government. Her politics stayed in the middle of the road, and she gained a reputation for grandstanding and playing to both sides of an issue.

Campus radicals remember Kim as a right-winger. "We were bitter opponents on student council at UBC," says Stan Persky, a writer and professor of political philosophy who was then the leading left-wing student on campus. "She looked to me like a straight right-winger with fluffy blond hair and well dressed and I thought: 'Oh, God. Here's the ancient regime.'" However, the moderates say she flirted with the left and was never right of centre. Don Mouton, who served as a vice-president of the Alma Mater Society with Kim, does not recall that she was particularly conservative. The right-wing voices came from the engineering students, says Mouton, now a professor of political science at UBC. Most other students, including Campbell, were reluctant to be tagged with a conservative label. "It just wasn't the time," he explains. "It was the height of protests against the war. No one would admit to being a conservative."

In an interview with Newman, Campbell confessed that she was unsure of her political philosophy in her undergraduate days. The socialists on campus were well motivated but highly unrealistic, while the Liberals appeared to be interested only in advancing their careers. "I was a Conservative in that I was certainly not a Liberal and I was not a Socialist," she said. She was also not very concerned with national politics, even though those were interesting times, when Canadians were enthralled by the rise of Quebec nationalism and the charisma of Pierre Trudeau. Few of the courses she took dealt with Canadian politics. She readily admits that she didn't really have a sense of the tensions in the country between English and French until 1967.

Campbell did, however, have an amazing ability to grab hold of hot issues that would boost her profile and popularity among students. When Persky, who headed the Arts Undergraduate Society, asked for a $5,000 loan from the student council to produce an anti-calendar, she was an enthusiastic backer. Persky's idea was to sell the calendar, which would feature a student evaluation of professors. Unfortunately, the calendar did not sell well and Persky could not repay the loan. A storm of protest ensued when the Alma Mater Society refused to give the Arts Society any more money in that year's budget. Campbell allied herself with Persky, much to the dismay of her AMS colleagues. At a raucous AMS meeting in Brock Hall attended by many angry students, Campbell spoke in favor of Persky, to the delight of the largely long-haired radical audience. "My firm recollection was that Kim came to that meeting when we discussed it and denounced the lack of money for Arts," says Mouton. Campbell's defection on this issue was particularly annoying to AMS councillors, since she tended to be present at their meetings only when the agenda was likely to garner headlines in the *Ubyssey*.

Another example of Campbell's flirtation with the left involved a controversy about freedom of expression. When Daniel Stoffman, now a business writer for *The Globe and Mail*, was the editor of the *Ubyssey*, the paper preached a radical line, often taking aim at the moderates on the student council. Campbell threatened to resign in protest when the AMS made a move to fire Stoffman for publishing an article containing obscene language. "We are both, and should be, a hotbed of revolutionary activity and a bastion of conservatism," she said. "The university is a place where everybody should be free." Mouton interprets Campbell's stance as "another example of Kim supporting the left-wing on campus rather as a kind of libertarian position on freedom of speech." Years later, Campbell told *Chatelaine* that although she "sympathized with the social concerns of campus activists," she "could not accept their leftist dogma."

Kim graduated from UBC in the spring of 1969 with an honors B.A. in political science. Her marks were good but certainly not outstanding. Although Campbell has many intellectual achievements to her credit, she did not always apply her considerable talents to her academic work. Too often she spread herself too thin. "She was a good student, but keep in mind she was also very heavily involved in student politics," comments Professor Kal Holsti, who taught Campbell as an undergraduate. "I have no hesitation in saying she was extremely bright, and when she applied herself, she did very good quality work. But she was involved in so many things that she was not always applying herself as much as she could have."

Lissa, who had married Bill soon after his divorce became final, flew in from Grenada with her husband for the graduation ceremonies. It was the first time Kim had seen her mother in ten years. Lissa and Bill had spent the last four years in the West Indies crewing a 60-foot chartered yacht for Philadelphia millionaire Adrian Hooper. Rich American tourists would fly into Grenada for ten days of luxury sailing, with Bill as captain and Lissa cooking sumptuous meals. Although Kim still harbored some resentment, she was delighted to see her mother. The two got along very well, although Lissa was not impressed by Tuzie. "I found him rude and pushy," she says. "I didn't like his personality at all."

The next year, Lissa and Bill returned to Canada permanently. They purchased a small oceanside home at Saratoga on Vancouver Island, on the Strait of Georgia. Bill got a job selling real estate in nearby Campbell River. Both Kim and Alix visited frequently. During the first Christmas they all spent together, Tuzie was the cause of some friction between Kim and her mother. Lissa recalls that Kim had told her Tuzie really wanted to celebrate with them: "She said, 'Oh yes, he wants to learn about Christmas.' So Alix and her husband [David Allen] came. And you know, Tuzie sat there just like an anthropologist watching the natives at their curious rites. He never joined in anything. He had a beautiful voice and he wouldn't sing a Christmas carol." Kim's uncle Doug also thought that Divinsky was odd. "He was kind of strange. He would have dinner and then go down and sleep for about three hours and then get up about 11 or midnight and work through the night."

After her graduation, Campbell accompanied Tuzie to the University of Oregon, where he taught two summer courses. While he lectured to graduate students, Campbell took a fourth-year undergraduate course. They lived in a furnished apartment and entertained Divinsky's colleagues with their renditions of Gilbert and Sullivan operettas. Betty Niven, the wife of a now-retired math professor, says she noticed Campbell was very confident even though "they were not married yet."

One thing Campbell did not do from 1969 to 1970 was earn a master's degree, as some reporters have written. Journalist Charlotte Gray, whose in-depth article on Campbell as Justice minister appeared in *Chatelaine* in September 1990, says that the minister's office provided her with the information she published about Campbell's M.A. "I have absolutely no doubt I got that from official sources," Gray says. "She did not write to me to tell me that was wrong." Although Campbell worked on a master's degree at the Institute of International Relations in the fall of 1969, she never completed it. Her willingness to let the error stand for so long contrasts sharply with her habit of dashing off letters to the editor to correct what she considers journalists' mistakes. "I think when there are factual errors I have a responsibility to respond as a member of Parliament," she said in December 1992 in response to a question about her many letters to editors. "I have an obligation as an MP and cabinet minister to tell the truth to people."

In October 1970, Campbell left Vancouver to study at the London School of Economics after winning a Canada Council doctoral fellowship worth between $3,500 and $5,500 a year. During the early 1970s, when she was in England, her thinking about politics was heavily influenced by Leonard Schapiro, a renowned professor of political science who specialized in Soviet studies. Until his death in 1983, Schapiro was known for his clear, thoughtful books and articles about Russian politics. A great believer in pluralism and democracy, he considered communism in the Soviet Union to be severely detrimental to freedom and prosperity.

With Schapiro as her adviser, Campbell worked on a thesis about the process of political socialization during de-Stalinization. Kim's relationship with her teacher seemed ideal. "He thought the world of her," says businessman Abe Sacks, Tuzie's partner in Bridges, a popular restaurant on Granville Island. Sacks took the two out to lunch when Schapiro was in Vancouver in the late 1970s. "She really respected him and he respected her," he says.

Schapiro's teachings about the pitfalls of highly centralized government were reinforced when Campbell toured the Soviet Union for three months in 1972 on a travel grant from the Canada Council. The long line-ups for food, the lack of consumer goods, the rampant alcoholism and the drabness of communist living made a deep impression on her. "I don't believe in a centrally planned economy because I don't think any planner can engineer a society [without] diminishing people's self-reliance," she later explained.

Aside from mentioning the work of Schapiro and Plato, Campbell has said in some interviews that the writings of Edmund Burke, the great eighteenth-century Whig statesman, have influenced the way she approaches politics. Burke, who is generally looked upon as the father of modern conservative theory, believed that government should be principled and tolerant, that tradition, law and morality should be respected and that a country's talented elites should be allowed to lead. His most famous utterance prescribes the proper attitude for members of Parliament. "Parliament is not a congress of ambassadors from different and hostile interests," he said in his 1774 Speech to the

Electors of Bristol, "but parliament is a deliberative assembly of one nation, with one interest, that of the whole; where, not local purposes, not local prejudices ought to guide, but the general good, resulting from the general reason of the whole. You choose a member indeed; but when you have chosen him, he is not a member of Bristol, but he is a member of parliament."

Campbell aligns herself with Burke in a general sense. "I would consider myself a political moderate, very much in the political centre, say . . . in the tradition of Burkean Conservatives," she told a CBC interviewer. "I see society as organic, not composed of separate independent individuals but as composed of interrelationships. I see human beings as imperfect. Therefore I don't think the role of government is to try to create a utopian perfect society. It is to try to create order and harmony." Often, she minimizes the influence that any one political theorist has had upon her. "I wouldn't note any political thinkers who influenced me in particular," she told Peter C. Newman. "I always knew I was a conservative, although I didn't really know why until later."

On September 15, 1972, Divinsky and Campbell were married in London while he was a visiting professor at Queen Mary College at the University of London. She was 25; he was 47. George and his third wife, family court intake officer Marguerite Parkinson, flew over to attend the ceremony. Although Lissa and Bill were absent, Kim paid for the trip of her grandmother Elizabeth. The energetic matriarch of the Cook family was eager for the adventure. At the age of 62, she had returned to teaching, travelling throughout British Columbia to native reserves and wherever else teachers were needed.

Instead of taking a honeymoon alone, the newlyweds hired a car and drove Elizabeth on a tour of Scotland. When they arrived in Wishal, Elizabeth's home town, she met an old man on the street where she used to play. "When I was a wee lassie the Gray girls gave me a farewell. Do they still live here?" she asked him. "Yes, indeed," said the old man. Elizabeth knocked on their door and became reacquainted with the two sisters, who had never married. "It made Mother sad," recalls Lissa. "Here she was with a wonderful granddaughter, and those old women who had never married, like a whole generation of women, because of World War I."

Soon after the wedding, Divinsky's two youngest daughters, Mimi and Pammie, came to London to stay for the year. From this visit Campbell would later say that she was a stepmother who had created a loving home for her husband's children. Betty Divinsky disagrees: "She spent one year with them in England, just with two of them. My oldest daughter didn't go, and they came back with a few problems. . . . She was a good friend to my youngest daughter, who was barely 12 when she went to England, but I think it is a habit Ms. Campbell has to blow up a small piece of information into something huge."

Students from British Columbia who attended the London School of Economics with Campbell remember her as being aloof. She would rarely join them in the pubs or take an active social interest as she had at UBC. Aside from her family and her studies, her main interests were the theatre and the London Symphony. Lyall Knott, a Vancouver resident who was studying for a master's in law at LSE, recalls that Campbell appeared not to be concerned with domestic politics. "She was not interested in Canadian partisan politics. I was involved in Canadian partisan politics with the Conservatives," he says. "I don't think she had any partisan politics. I remember going down to Canada House with a bunch of my buddies on election night in 1972 and she was not there."

Campbell returned to Canada in 1973 without completing her doctoral thesis. She immediately applied for a teaching position in political science at Simon Fraser University and was turned down, though she was hired for part-time lecturing. She told Charlotte Gray that "not only had they hired an American man but they'd even lost my résumé." In a speech to women journalists in November 1992, she described universities as the "last bastion of great sexism in this country," perhaps as a way of explaining why she did not succeed in academia. While it is true that statistically Canadian universities are sexist in their hiring practices, it is also true that a person of either sex with neither an M.A. nor a Ph.D. is very unlikely to find a position. "I had heard that she was a little bit miffed about not being able to get a full-time job at the university," says Professor Holsti. "The chances of her doing it without a degree would have been fairly slight."

Campbell also tends to exaggerate her ability to speak several languages. While she can speak a very serviceable French, people have questioned claims in her official biography that she is fluent in Russian and German. "Her Russian is almost non-existent and her German is probably worse," J. J. Camp, a friend and former head of the Canadian Bar Association, told Canadian Press. In 1993, she said that she picked up some Yiddish from Tuzie, lengthening the list of languages with which she has claimed to be familiar.

For two years after she came back from London, Campbell seemed to enjoy being a homemaker for Tuzie. The couple lived in a rambling house near the UBC campus with their dog. She did not appear to be pursuing a career. No one could understand why she never completed her doctorate. "That was a real mystery because the horsepower was there," says Abe Sacks.

In May 1993, Campbell explained to Peter O'Neil of *The Vancouver Sun* that other activities took her away from her doctoral project. "I was working very hard every year preparing new courses and it also became very apparent that I wasn't going to be able to get a permanent academic position. And it began to make less and less sense for me to try and finish my thesis. It happens to a lot of people. I just got away from it, doing other work."

Campbell loved to cook and to entertain Tuzie's business and academic friends. Once, all on her own, she prepared an outdoor dinner for a group of 80 visiting mathematicians. She adopted the dress, attitudes and even eating habits of her husband's older friends. "She made a major effort to make the marriage work," recalls one friend. Tuzie could be very domineering because of his sheer energy. He would play the piano in the morning, chess in the afternoon and bridge at night. But, although he was a busy man, he was very good to Kim in many ways. He encouraged her to learn the cello, to read stimulating books, to discuss world events and to debate ideas. Friends insist that he did not try to limit her by demanding that she play the perfect wife. It was her choice.

Campbell seemed totally devoted to Tuzie's projects. In 1974 she worked to get him elected to the Vancouver School Board, where he eventually became chairman. She was also involved in his efforts to develop the university's endowment lands. As president of UBC's Non-Profit Building Society, Tuzie created 69 units worth more than $4 million. "The only difference between me and a developer was that I worked for nothing," he once said.

Between 1975 and 1978, Campbell worked as a part-time lecturer at UBC, filling in for professors on sabbatical. In the first year she taught Contemporary Ideology 202 and a fourth-year course on Soviet and Eastern European politics. In the 1977–78 term, she repeated 202 and instructed second-year students in a course on international politics. "She was a superb classroom teacher, really a superb teacher. She took an interest in students," says UBC professor Paul Tennant. One of Campbell's students, Carolyn Phillips remembers the kindness Campbell showed when she was seriously injured in a car accident. Bedridden and unable to write the final exam, Phillips might have lost a year had Campbell not been willing to bend the rules to allow an oral examination.

In the late seventies, Campbell faced a number of emotional crises. In 1978 she wanted to have a child and felt exuberant about planning a pregnancy. When Bill Vroom had open-heart surgery that year, Kim rushed over to the Island to comfort her mother. "Kim was telling all the old men about the baby she was going to have," recalls Lissa. "Bill said, 'What a cutie she is.' Those were his last words about her." Bill died 24 hours later when the stitching let go. "My sister saw him a few hours before he died," says Doug Cook. "He said, 'Well, I just got back from the dead. I'm living on free time. Let's sell the house, buy a yacht and go to Tahiti and live the rest of our lives down there.'" Two hours later Bill's heart gave out and Lissa lost the man who had given her nearly 20 years of happiness.

Kim never gave birth to a child. Lissa says that her daughter was told by doctors that she "could not conceive." A friend of the family says there was "great sadness" in the household at that time and that Campbell became "rather listless" when she was not able to have a child. She and Tuzie began to drift apart. "There must have been a growing frustration with the disparity of age and not having children and looking after children about her same age," says a friend of those years. Kim began to put on a lot of weight and to age, almost taking on the physical characteristics of Tuzie's social circle.

Reeling from the emotional effects of both Bill's death and the news about her infertility, Campbell received a third shock when Alix's husband, David Allen, died at the age of 32. A physical education teacher in West Vancouver, Allen had come home from a girls' basketball game while Alix was studying for her final law exams. "He had come back and he was very happy. He went to the washroom to wash his hands and she heard a crash. She ran in and he was dead," says Aunt Shirley. "You know what? He never smoked, never drank and they both jogged and ate healthy food." Alix performed CPR on David until an ambulance arrived, but it was too late. For months afterwards she had terrible nightmares and relied on Kim and Lissa for comfort.

Life had begun to inflict some cruel blows on Campbell, whose future had looked so promising when she graduated from UBC a decade earlier. Without an advanced degree, she was unable to continue finding course work at her alma mater. Although she was hired to lecture at night on international relations and political philosophy at Vancouver Community College's Langara campus, she was turned down for a full-time position there in 1979. Seeing that she was deeply discouraged with academia, Abe Sacks urged her to go into law. "I could see it in her—that it might have been more of a challenge to get out in reality."

3

AMBITIONS

Passion for fame; a passion which is the instinct of
all great souls.

—*Edmund Burke*

L aw school offered Kim Campbell a chance for rebirth. For too
long her social circle had been restricted to people of her parents' generation. Now her new career path brought her into daily
contact with a vibrant group of younger people whose minds and
lifestyles enlivened her spirit. At age 32, Campbell was about ten
years older than most students in the class of 1980. However, despite this age difference, she blossomed among the people and the
challenges, just as she had at St. Ann's, Prince of Wales and UBC.

Like many women who return to school after a hiatus at home,
Campbell earned high grades. Although she had all the skills
needed to fit into the academic milieu, her classmates noticed that
she seemed to belong to another generation. Her hair was cut in a
bouffant and she never wore the youthful styles that would have

put her in harmony with campus fashion. Occasionally, when she did wear blue jeans, her friends thought she looked more attractive. Nevertheless, no matter how she dressed, Campbell's enthusiasm, ambition and vitality made her an appealing presence. Classmate Rachel Campbell, daughter of the former mayor of Vancouver, remembers that Kim's energy was palpable. "She was just always smiling and always running around school, laughing and organizing. She had her hand in everything."

Tuzie is said to have been worried about his wife's lethargy before she entered law school. She had always been a person who needed adulation, and he knew that she still had a powerful drive to be seen as successful. In many ways he was just like her; he needed to continually prove himself by surmounting new challenges.

By 1980, Tuzie was no longer interested in the Vancouver School Board. He was tired of fighting pitched battles with COPE, the Committee of Progressive Electors, a group of left-leaning trustees who tended to belong to the New Democratic Party. COPE encouraged the advancement of women as school principals and supported programs for children who had learning disabilities or who were otherwise disadvantaged by poverty and family break-ups. Such an agenda often clashed with that of Divinsky's camp, the electors of the Civic Non-Partisan Association, known as the NPA, who reflected the business community's views on education by focussing on decreasing the burdens on taxpayers and promoting a back-to-basics approach to curriculum development. The rancor displayed at board meetings between COPE and the NPA was legendary.

After four years as chairman of the school board, Tuzie decided to become an alderman, declaring that he was putting his name forward in the fall municipal election to pry the city loose from the socialist moralists and to raise the level of debate by "talking to the point and trying to get to the heart of the matter." Convinced that his wife would be the best person to replace him, Tuzie urged Kim to seek one of the nine school board trustee nominations for the NPA. He had no doubt that she could handle the pressures of the board as well as the rigorous demands of law school.

On October 3, 1980, Campbell easily won the nomination with her husband's help. Her campaign literature claimed that she was a graduate of the London School of Economics. However, no matter what she said in her promotional material, her greatest advantage in the fall election was her last name. Paul Tennant, professor of urban studies at UBC, notes that because Vancouver has no wards and up to 35 people running for the school board, "if you are early in the alphabet you've got a much better chance. So C for Campbell is just the perfect place on the ballot." After the fall election, COPE formed the majority for the first time in years while the NPA won only three seats.

Campbell assumed her $6,000-a-year post when British Columbia's educational system was in tumult. The provincial government in Victoria was led by tough-talking Premier Bill Bennett, a neo-conservative cut from the same cloth as Ronald Reagan. A devotee of the right-wing Fraser Institute, which had launched a frontal attack on the welfare state and a bloated bureaucracy, Bennett saw educators as a drain on taxpayers' dollars. To his way of thinking, teachers had it soft with their long summer vacations, frequent holidays and fat paycheques. The fact that teachers' salaries were rising while enrolment was dropping after the overcrowded decades of the baby boomers made Bennett's position credible to many in the province.

In 1981, teachers, arguing that inflation was out of control, wrested a 17 percent salary hike for the next school year. Bennett was incensed. Although, according to Statistics Canada, educational costs in B.C. as a percentage of personal income were about even with Ontario at 8.7 percent and much lower than cash-strapped Newfoundland at 12.3 percent, Bennett and his followers saw the teachers as greedy feeders at the public trough.

The cause of the troubles facing Campbell and the other trustees was the severity of the recession that had crushed Vancouver's red-hot housing market as interest rates rocketed to 20 percent. When thousands of workers lost their jobs because the province's resource industries were unable to sell their products, there was a ripple effect throughout the economy. Bankruptcies soared while inflation gobbled up any wage gains made by those who were lucky enough to still have jobs. Taxpayers were biting the bullet and wondering why the cost of public education had soared to $1.6 billion from 1976 even though there were now 32,000 fewer students. It was the worst of times to be charged with the responsibility for the school system.

The Vancouver School Board would become a microcosm of the battle between left and right that raged throughout the province. The 1981 minutes of meetings of the board chaired by socialist Pauline Weinstein show that left-wing trustees had little interest in trying to curtail spending. In debates about the 1982 financial plan, Campbell led the conservative forces seeking to trim a $175-million budget of which 86 percent went to pay teachers and staff. Conceding that she could be accused of being "anti-child," the new trustee argued that in real dollars the board was spending twice as much per child as it had in the 1950s. "I am concerned that the school board is the only public body able to use a blank cheque," she said in November. "Public spending has gotten out of control at all levels."

COPE trustees naturally disliked Campbell and her constant complaints about the plight of taxpayers. In response to her concern about overspending, trustee Wes Knapp countered that the cut-and-slash talk threatened a program set up to combat racism as well as initiatives to help native children and the needy. "We're not advocating wild, slashing cuts," countered Campbell. "But let's maintain the status quo. On the basis of 1,600 fewer students than last year, that would not make a Simon Legree budget." The records demonstrate that she was the one consistent advocate of fiscal restraint on the board.

In contrast to her days at UBC, Campbell was more willing to tackle left-wing rhetoric head on. In one debate, COPE trustees got sidetracked from school board business to express their outrage over a decision by the board of Vancouver Community College to deny enrolment to 15 students sponsored by the Libyan government of Moammar Qaddafi. Trustee Gary Onstad noted that the battleship USS *Ranger* was in port. "One of the biggest symbols of terrorism is in our harbor and we don't turn down U.S. students," he declared to a sympathetic audience. "What if they're sent here by the CIA?" Campbell quipped, much to the annoyance of Weinstein, who insisted that "they have a right to speak. That's our policy."

In her earlier political activities, Campbell had been careful not to offend too many people. A clever politician who played to the crowds, she was always respected and popular. Now, some people saw a marked transformation in her political personality. "She was rude and arrogant and just hopeless in terms of dealing with underlings like superintendents of schools," says Phil Rankin, an assertive left-leaning lawyer and trustee who frequently clashed with Campbell. "She's a terrible bully. She would upbraid people regularly and just try to shit on them before they got a chance to finish." Knapp characterized Campbell as a "bull in a china shop" with a terrible temper.

Not everyone who served on the school board with Campbell accepts Rankin's and Knapp's assessments of her. NPA trustee Jonathan Baker said her impatience was understandable in light of the board's irresponsible attitude to public finances and the constant ranting of left-wing supporters. "There were times when we would go to board meetings or public hearings and the teachers' association would pack the meetings, and you'd have 700 people screaming at you," he told *The Vancouver Sun*. "She was often faced with a strident, hostile and angry audience." Undoubtedly Campbell had reason, on occasion, to lose her temper. But Paul Tennant, whose academic specialty is local government, says she displayed an attitude that could be grating. "If she's got a failing, it's that she doesn't suffer fools gladly. And she certainly would, at times, be critical of officials, critical of pressure groups and spokespersons before the school board."

The haughtiness that had been so unlike Campbell in her high-school and UBC days can be partly attributed to the influence of Nathan Divinsky. A friend who socialized with the couple during those years says she imitated her husband: "She developed the arrogant thinking of Tuzie. He tended to act superior to most of the people he met." In a politically charged atmosphere she responded by dismissing her opponents as intellectual lightweights just as Divinsky had done when he served as chairman of the board. In addition, one acquaintance suggests that Campbell's years of association with academics led her to adopt a certain intellectual bravado.

In social settings, however, Campbell was warm, witty, animated and attentive. Leah Sacks remembers that Campbell was eager to share creative recipes from her successful dinner party menus. And, when Sacks's daughter was struggling with a term paper, Campbell devoted an hour to explain how to write an A-plus essay. "From that time forward my daughter got the best of marks," says Sacks. Law school classmates and professors also saw a different Campbell than the hot-tempered trustee of the right. "She wasn't a show-off ever. She was surprisingly modest," recalls Rachel Campbell. She even won over Paisley Woodward, a leftist law student. When Campbell first entered second-year property class, Woodward had yelled "Hurrah COPE!" as a taunt because Kim's opponents had just won a majority on the school board. Eventually, however, the two women became close friends despite their different political leanings. Campbell once went to a party at Woodward's where she played the guitar and sang to the rather startled left-wing crowd.

Although the return to law school breathed new life into Kim, it strained her relationship with Tuzie because she had less time for him and his world of theatre, dinner parties, chess and bridge. She revelled in the company of her younger friends, hoisting glasses with them at the weekly "beer-ups." She wrote outrageous satires for the "Law Revue," an evening of music and skits that poked fun at the legal and political establishment. Friends observed that she began to lose weight and to flirt with other men. "She shed so many years and got so much younger," says one of Tuzie's colleagues. Another recalls that "she started a life of her own, with younger people, and you could see they were just strangers passing in the night."

While Campbell was making new friends, Tuzie was quickly becoming known as an uncaring buffoon at city hall. In January 1981 he was widely criticized for opposing a plan requiring a developer to designate five units out of 50 for social housing. "Why should developers be required to subsidize housing for low-income people?" he argued. Divinsky liked to be noticed. Putting half-eaten apples on his desk and working on contract bridge puzzles during intense discussions were two of his favorite ways of drawing attention to himself during meetings. "He's a buffoon," Alderman Harry Rankin told *The Vancouver Sun* that year. Often Rankin would lose his temper and tell the diminutive professor to "shut up and sit down."

The Vancouver Sun described Divinsky as the council clown: "He likes to crack jokes and make light out of a heavy discussion, but too often his humor borders on the insensitive. . . . When he's not joking, he gives loud, long flowery speeches illustrating his positions." Campbell's embarrassment at Tuzie's behavior may also have been a factor in their break-up.

Friends say that Tuzie kept a "stiff upper lip" as his second marriage deteriorated. Not one to wallow in self-pity, he seemed to harbor hope that this was just a phase. But, after much reflection,

Campbell finally decided to leave her husband and mentor of nine years. In January 1982, she moved into a rented condominium in the neighborhood of False Creek. Family and friends were informed that the two had simply grown apart. "It was very, very traumatic for me. I felt a great sense of failure," Campbell said. Although he was hurt, Divinsky put on a happy face. "He's the kind of guy who would not want to be a crybaby," says a friend.

When the final divorce papers were filed in Chilliwack in August 1983, Campbell was left in a strong financial position. She received 5 percent non-voting shares in Jalm Holdings, the company that owns Bridges. Established by Divinksy with four partners in 1979, the Granville Island restaurant was a huge success. During the busy summer season its cash registers rake in more than $1 million each month. Campbell's share, which she sold in 1989, was worth over $100,000. Also as part of the settlement, the couple's house was sold, and she used that money to put a down payment on a $210,000 stylish house in Fairview Slopes. It is now worth approximately $550,000.

Campbell insists that her relationship with Tuzie ended amicably and that they remain friends to this day. However, Divinsky made several revealing comments when Campbell announced that she was running for the leadership of the federal Conservatives. Their relationship, he told Holly Horwood of *The Province*, "had a range of aspects from wonderful to mediocre to horrible." Horwood reported that Divinsky acknowledged Campbell was capable, intelligent and witty. Then he paused. "The trouble is when you're married you see everything. You see the person not only physically naked but mentally naked. If I need some money, I could write a book. I have pictures . . . I'm planning on getting a bumper sticker that says, 'I Screwed the Prime Minister.'" Although his comments say more about him than they do about Campbell, the remarks indicate that on his part there is little friendship left between him and his second ex-wife.

The same month that Campbell left Tuzie, Premier Bennett gathered his top cabinet ministers and civil servants at Schooner Cove, on Vancouver Island, to discuss the spiralling cost of education and a public-service sector that was out of control. On February 18, Bennett went live on province-wide television to unveil a wage restraint program. Generous by today's standards, but just keeping pace with inflation in 1982, Bennett's program kept public-sector wage hikes to between 8 and 14 percent. Spending on schools, hospitals and municipalities was limited to an increase of 12 percent.

Bennett's policies created a crisis for schools across the province. Boards were being ordered to revise their budgets to meet the 12 percent ceiling, although teachers had just negotiated a 17 percent raise. Layoffs were a foregone conclusion. Vancouver's school board was required to trim $2 million from its budget in 1982 and $4 million in 1983. In March, Bennett added to the woe by decreeing that henceforth school boards could tax only residences and not commercial or industrial property. Dominated by COPE, the Vancouver School Board reacted by declaring a hiring freeze and challenging the legality of the restraint program. The court ruled in favor of Victoria and the school board was forced to slash $4 million from its budget.

Worse punishment came in August when Bennett shifted Bill Vander Zalm over to the Education portfolio. In his previous post, at Municipal Affairs, Vander Zalm had made headlines by bashing welfare programs and slashing local governments. Now Bennett was setting him loose to trample on B.C.'s already troubled education system. Children should learn to "write good," he said shortly after taking office. Vander Zalm tabled the government's restraint bill in the fall—an action that cost teachers five days' pay. He then axed six professional-development days from the school calendar and suspended any contract that was in conflict with the legislation.

At the board, Campbell weighed in on the side of the Social Credit Party, blasting the teachers for preferring to reduce the budget for substitute teachers instead of cancelling professional-development days. She pointed to the "hypocrisy" of the teachers' association for rejecting layoffs of its own members, while allowing substitutes to bear the brunt of cuts. While Wes Knapp and other COPE trustees defended the teachers by saying they should not be blamed for the high wage settlement, Campbell decried their stance as the "unacceptable face of trade unionism." She presented herself as a realist. The Socreds were going to impose the cuts in any case, and the mandate of the board was to manage the education system with the money available. Her position did not win her many friends among either teachers or trade unionists.

The debate over restraint was not the only hot topic facing the school board in 1982. Though it was not directly school board business, Campbell and Jonathan Baker locked swords with COPE over the development of B.C. Place lands on the north shore of False Creek. Trustees had voted six to two in support of city council's plan to provide social housing on the site. Baker said the proposal was "like planning to feed a hungry crowd with a case of caviar." He thought B.C. Place should be kept for singles and seniors to avoid "ghettos of subsidized housing." COPE's Michael O'Neill accused Campbell and Baker of wanting to keep the West End a community where "children are not wanted and are seen as a liability."

"I resent Trustee O'Neill's statements," snapped Campbell in an angry exchange in June.

"Not surprising," interjected Phil Rankin.

"Put a can in it, Rankin," she shouted.

"This is the lowest level of debate that this school board has had in two years," interjected Gary Onstad. "Gutter talk . . . get it out of this school board."

In general, Campbell preferred that the school board stay out of matters that concerned the business community. Her approach was evident in the disagreement she had with Frank Dingman of the Alcohol and Drug Education Service in July. Dingman was seeking support to protest the lifting of a 30-year ban on beer and wine advertising on TV on the grounds that the ads encouraged alcoholism. "A lot of people are complaining about the [social] cost of these ads," he said. "It's not too late to turn it around. Premier Bennett is the only one who can turn it around and it has to be done immediately." Campbell challenged Dingman, insisting that there was no link between alcoholism and TV ads. "In the U.S.S.R. they have the highest incidence of alcohol problems without any advertising at all," she said. "This could have the opposite effect—besides, it's basically a brand-name competition. There's more control if the advertising money stays here than if it goes across the border as it does now—beamed back here without any controls."

In the fall, Campbell decided to seek another term on the school board, though she was still pursuing her law studies. At an all-candidates meeting in late October, Campbell distanced herself from the Bennett regime. "It gives me a pain in the ass, you'll pardon the expression, to be called a Socred," she proclaimed. Allen Garr, columnist for *The Province*, was awestruck. "Campbell melted her microphone and raised the cavernous room's temperature to near comfort," he wrote, correctly noting that the "NPA are the long-time civic soulmates of the Socreds. Their party colors and their candidates are as interchangeable as their bagmen."

During the election, other NPA candidates found Campbell's behavior frustrating because she behaved like a chameleon, changing her views to fit the audience. They say that one moment she was on their side, but, five minutes later, she was singing out of a different songbook; it all depended on the crowd. Ken Denike, a UBC specialist in agriculture running for the NPA, remembers the first all-candidates forum, at Point Grey School. "I thought we had agreement on the general areas we were going to take. We went into the general meeting and were on stage, and by the luck of the draw, she was the first of the three of us to speak. It turned out to be the opposite position." Denike got to the point where he did not want to go on stage with her. "To put it mildly, there was a degree of concern every time she stood up on the stage."

At times Campbell also angered her NPA colleagues with her unpredictability. Denike recalls an example. In mid-November he drew up an NPA plan to avoid layoffs and a rollback of teachers' wages in the new budget crunch imposed by Victoria that fall. The province stipulated that the Vancouver School Board budget be set at $165 million. The NPA suggested that the trustees overcome the $10-million shortfall by dipping into the board's $11-million capital surplus fund created by the sale of property. The plan was to take $4.5 million out of the fund and ask the provincial government for a matching contribution. Initially, Campbell supported the idea. Then she spoke against it.

Annoyed at her flip-flops, Denike and his NPA colleagues met with her, and all agreed to speak as one voice. At a news conference on November 15, the five NPA candidates—including Campbell—announced that they were seeking Vander Zalm's approval of their restraint package. Because he was aware of Campbell's mercurial nature, Denike had written a script for each candidate to present to the media. "She did it faithfully," he recalls. "Thereafter the issue would come up and you'd think it was her idea. She used almost the same words, which I obviously recognized. I had written them."

COPE trustees presumed their fierce opposition to Socred cost-cutting would ensure them an easy ride to victory. They were sadly mistaken. Vander Zalm was far more in tune with an electorate lashed by the recession and crying for tax relief. Voters throughout the province favored cuts in spending. Six NPA candidates swept the race in Vancouver. Campbell, the loudest voice for restraint, topped the polls and was immediately elected chair of the board.

Campbell tackled her task with a vengeance. Faced with the budget crunch inflicted by Victoria, she was determined to slash elective programs such as drama and music in order to preserve basic courses and jobs. She seemed to prefer sacrificing programs that affected the poor rather than those that affected the middle class. In February the NPA pushed through a motion to impose user fees for all summer programs and slapped a $10 levy on all supplies for elementary students. Poor children having to make up courses or not having the $10 could apply for a handout. COPE's Pauline Weinstein warned that user fees would be an extra financial burden on 48,000 welfare recipients and the city's 78,000 unemployed. "It's one more kick in the pants," she said.

Campbell explained that fees for summer programs would be charged just to those seeking advanced academic standing. Fellowships would be offered to poor students who attended summer school to make up for failed courses. Knapp pointed out that it was clear from Campbell's statement that she thought low-income children were not smart enough for the advanced programs. He reminded her that there were also children from impoverished homes who wanted to take courses to advance their academic standing.

In March 1983, the school board reduced health services in the schools, including a popular immunization program. "We looked for some areas to cut back because of restraint and we were the only district that was doing it," Campbell said. "We might have done it even if there was no restraint. It's ridiculous to provide these services when you can get it free in the community. Why spend scarce education dollars?" She added that it would be cheaper to charter a bus and take the kids to the nearest medical centre. Denike said that Campbell's position was akin to arguing that school lunches should not be provided for hungry children from deprived homes.

Despite her enthusiasm for restraint, Campbell managed to find enough money to institute an International Baccalaureate program for gifted children. She argued that although there were plenty of programs for disabled or disadvantaged students, there were few for the truly talented. The new program offered intensive studies for exceptionally bright children that would help open the door to almost any university in the world. Although the program proved successful, it reinforced, with COPE, Campbell's image as an elitist. "She has no feeling at all for the underprivileged," fumed Phil Rankin.

COPE also felt that the NPA had little sympathy for gays or for the children of immigrants. While Campbell chaired the board, funds were reduced for courses in English as a second language and nothing was done to inform children about the danger of AIDS. The federal government, she argued, should pick up the tab for language training since it is in charge of immigration. As for AIDS, that was a moral issue outside the purview of the schools. There was hardly an issue on which left and right could agree.

Although Campbell was confrontational with COPE trustees and teachers, her style of dealing with Bill Vander Zalm was pragmatic. "I'm not going to back away," she once said. "But the reality is that he has the power and the money, and if getting what I want makes him look good I'm prepared to make him look good." Her first major initiative was a budget calling for layoffs of up to 457 employees, including 224 teachers—a figure that was later pared down to 194 teachers and 28 counsellors, administrators and special-needs experts.

Board politics consumed Campbell and gave her less time to pursue her law studies. Like many law students, she cut corners by sharing notes and cramming for exams. Although she had been in the top 15 percent of her class in her first year, her marks fell off in the second and third years. Nonetheless, she impressed her law professors with her powerful intellect and upbeat attitude. George Curtis, the 86-year-old dean emeritus of the faculty who taught Kim, Alix and George, remembers Kim as a real joy: "She had a first-rate mind and a very pleasant manner. She handled herself well in discussion." Professor Barry Slutsky also found Campbell to be "always a bright, articulate, fun-loving person" who was very confident in a "male-dominated place from both a teacher's and student's perspective."

In her last year, she wrote, produced and directed the 1983 "Law Revue"—an evening of satire that focussed on the split between the left- and right-wing factions of the school board. The second part of the revue was a musical farce she called "The Best Little Courthouse in Canada." Her script adopted styles from the popular SCTV late-night comedy show of the early 1980s. "It was particularly funny that year and she was particularly responsible for putting it together," recalls Professor Keith Farquhar. Despite her conservative views, Farquhar says she could poke fun at herself and few students held a "negative view about her."

Premier Bennett and his chief lieutenant, Patrick Kinsella, were impressed by Campbell's politics. Articulate and dynamic, she was a voice of restraint on the school board and a proven vote-getter. Bennett thought she might have the right stuff for a special mission. In the next election, he was determined to dethrone Gary Lauk, an NDP member of the legislature. Lauk and Emery Barnes had held the two-member riding of Vancouver Centre for the NDP since 1972. Lauk had particularly enraged both the Socreds and the business establishment a year earlier when he erroneously told the legislature that the Canadian Imperial Bank of Commerce was on the brink of receivership. He was forced to apologize when his remarks caused a run on the Canadian dollar and sent CIBC shares tumbling.

Vancouver Centre was a microcosm of the city's diversity. The riding encompassed wealthy enclaves, slums and highrises, and was home to blue-collar workers, entrepreneurs, senior citizens, transients, gays and ethnic minorities. Most of the hot issues affecting the city—such as prostitution, high rents, downtown development, B.C. Place lands and rapid transit—fell within the riding's boundaries.

When Bennett called a spring election in 1984, Campbell agreed to run for the Socreds in the Vancouver Centre riding, despite her earlier pronouncement that it gave her a "pain in the ass" to be associated with the party of the right. Her running mate, businessman and former Parks Board chairman Phil Owen, was not considered a strong candidate because he had lost a bid for alderman in the 1982 municipal election. Campbell immediately ran off to see Lyall Knott, a prominent lawyer and Tory organizer whom she knew from the London School of Economics. Knott was the key man in Tory minister Pat Carney's federal Vancouver Centre riding and commanded a formidable organization. "Kim dropped in to see me because she was looking for support from the Conservative organization," remembers Knott, who offered her campaign soldiers, lists of voters and advice about the location of lawn signs. Since she did not really need Tory support, her meeting with Knott demonstrated the extent of her thoroughness and determination.

Money from business—the mining sector in particular—poured into Socred coffers to bankroll the Campbell-Owen team in the effort to unseat Lauk. The Richard Street campaign headquarters had the latest in high-tech political gadgetry. They had sophisticated photocopiers, pagers for volunteers and banks of telephones. Bennett came into the riding regularly—once accompanied by a brass band and painted clowns—to whip up the Socred faithful. Lauk believes that the Socreds spent more than $300,000 in the riding.

The campaign was nasty, particularly in the downtown east side where the NDP ruled the roost. "My wife would campaign with Kim," recalls Knott, "and I remember Susan coming home and she would have been hit by a stick and she would have had things thrown at her." However, Campbell was no push-over. Lauk describes her as an "attack dog" who was "not there for the laughs." She worked very hard in her campaign, speaking at candidates meetings, pounding the pavement, knocking on doors and pressing the flesh. At every opportunity she decried the big-spending, New Deal socialists while promoting Socred projects in the riding, such as B.C. Place and Expo 86.

Although Campbell pleased audiences when she mentioned Socred efforts at job creation, few voters were impressed by her stand against the across-the-board rent controls that the NDP was effectively advocating in the downtown core. She was bruised when one of her organizers sent out fundraising letters to landlords in which she vowed to abolish rent controls cherished by the socialists. Lauk got hold of one of the letters and gleefully published it in the community newspapers. "I prefer to give up 12 landlord votes for 15,000 tenants," he joked.

The NDP used Campbell's occasional temper tantrums to great effect. "She was abrasive and, of course, at that stage in her career it was easy to press that button, and I did it at every opportunity. Every time she blew her cool at an all-candidates meeting I gained another 500 votes," admits Lauk. Campbell was often her own worst enemy. Lauk remembers a meeting at the Carnegie Centre, in the heart of skid row. The audience of several hundred was composed of many recovering alcoholics and welfare recipients who shopped regularly at Salvation Army stores. Lauk came dressed in a three-piece suit and a fashionable tie because he knew that this was how the crowd expected an MLA to look. Campbell dressed down, coming into the room in a pair of blue jeans and a mackinaw. He recalls that "she took the microphone and she said, 'I know many of you have had disappointments in your life. I have too. When I was a teenager I wanted to be a concert cellist.' We all sort of politely glazed over our eyes and looked out the venetian blinds."

Despite these gaffes, Campbell was by no means a write-off. She had an effective organization and the eager support of landlords and businesspeople. Because the New Democrats were worried, they enlisted the aid of Alderman Bill Yee to bring out the vote in Chinatown. "It's a genuine challenge," Campbell said a few days before the May 5 election. "I find it very hard to call. I know people say it is going to be a squeaker." When the ballots were counted, Campbell was trounced. She polled 9,938, compared with 15,008 for Lauk and 15,149 for Barnes. Owen was only 300 votes behind his star running mate.

The NDP took small comfort in the victory in Vancouver Centre. Bill Bennett swept the province, capturing 35 seats to the NDP's 22. Convinced that the Socreds had earned a "strong and enduring mandate," the premier launched what Allen Garr describes as the most radical revolution in B.C. history. In July he unveiled a budget that wiped out the independent human rights commission, abolished rent controls, permitted landlords to evict tenants without cause and removed tax credits for low-income renters and the elderly. The two-year sunset clause on wage controls was extended indefinitely and the government was given the authority to roll back salaries in the public sector. The bureaucracy was slashed by 25 percent.

Education was not spared in Bennett's Revolution of the Right. Four bills were tabled to raise teacher-pupil ratios substantially within three years. Layoffs were inevitable. Principals and other top administrators were classified as senior managers in a bid to divide the British Columbia Teachers' Federation. The most significant bill took the power to determine budgets away from the school boards and gave it to the bureaucrats in Victoria. The Premier's Office was now firmly in charge, erasing a century of local community control over schools. In his 1985 book *School Wars*, journalist Crawford Kilian wrote, "A whole level of government has been gutted. School trustees now have no serious powers. Their function for the next three years will be to preside over the dismantling of the system they have spent decades building."

Campbell saw nothing sinister in stripping local school boards of their powers. "They're doing the best they can in a difficult situation," she said. As for increasing the student-teacher ratio,

Campbell declared: "The most effective class I taught at university had 90 students." Other trustees did not consider the legislation so benign. They felt that while it was one thing to control spending, it was quite another to take complete control. "We now have the power of a parent-advisory board. It is the complete destruction of local autonomy and a complete destruction of bargaining power," said Bev Rodrigo, vice-president of the B.C. School Trustees Association. Even Gary Begin, a defeated Socred candidate and former trustees association president, was aghast at the legislation. "The plan to override locally elected boards threatens local government—one of the cornerstones of democracy." Begin declared that he would not have run under the Socred banner had he known about Bennett's intent to blitz the school system.

Teachers and public-service unions were furious at Bennett's savage approach to curbing public spending. The slashing of social services, the attacks on unions and the blatant disregard for collective bargaining rights unleashed a fire storm of protest across the province. Art Kube of the B.C. Federation of Labour and leaders of the B.C. Government Employees' Union formed Operation Solidarity to fight Bennett's reactionary policies. B.C. Teachers' Federation boss Larry Kuehn urged teachers to strike in the fall of that year. Three weeks later, Kuehn announced that 59.45 percent of the membership had voted in favor of a walkout. Some 16,162 teachers wanted to strike, while 11,025 were opposed. Although this was not an overwhelming mandate, Kuehn described it as "substantial" because so many teachers had voted to join the province-wide walkout knowing that their association was not recognized as a union and had no legal authority to strike.

When Campbell heard that the teachers were planning to strike, she told *The Province* that she hoped they "would get kicked in the ass." Two days later, at a heated school board meeting, trustee Pauline Weinstein called for the chair's resignation. An angry and defiant Campbell stood her ground. "I'm sorry, perhaps, that I used those words because they don't look very good in print, but the context in which they were spoken was completely distorted. I stated that I believed teachers did not have a legal right to strike and that I hoped that if and when the issue went to court that teachers would get kicked in the ass, and I did use that expression, but I used it with respect to what I thought was a desirable outcome of a legal proceeding resolving the issue." COPE's Weinstein remarked that Campbell's comments were typical of her "baseball-bat approach" to issues.

As the deadline for the teachers' strike approached, Campbell's rhetoric became more colorful. "It's typical terrorist tactics, the idea of getting what you want by holding innocent people hostage," she declared. Six days later, at a press conference, Campbell reacted to voters' strong criticism of her remark by using gentler language. "It would be a terrible mistake for our local boards to take an unbending position," she said. At times she admitted the government's program had been marked by "ineptitude and woolliness" but still insisted on backing Bennett. When she went to court to get an injunction to stop the strike, she won a temporary victory. In November, the teachers walked out for three days despite the disapproval of the courts.

In December, Campbell stepped down as chair of the board and announced that she would not seek a third term, stating that it was too difficult to juggle school board duties and complete the articling requirement for her law degree. "The time pressures make it impossible for me to continue to do the type of job I would like to do for the board," she explained. "The nights I'm not at the board, I'm at my firm."

Campbell was turned down when she sought a coveted position articling with Knott, Pollard and Morgan (now merged with Clark, Wilson). However, she was accepted by Ladner Downs, an equally prestigious firm where she hoped to become a lawyer specializing in commercial crime.

She soon grew bored at the big downtown firm. Friends say that she resented being treated like the other new lawyers and that she thought she deserved more challenging work. She was not assigned serious work and rarely got a chance to handle her own files. "I knew she was really frustrated at Ladner Downs because the work wasn't that interesting," says a lawyer who was one of Campbell's friends. "You do a little bit of work on one case—you draft an affidavit or do some research on it—but it's not really your field and you don't have contact with the client. I mean there she was, Kim Campbell, and they're saying fine, we don't care who you are. It wasn't a great fit."

It was time to look for a new challenge.

4

FANTASYLAND

If you look at Vander Zalm's appeal, it comes from the sense
that he tells it like it is. I don't understand that view. I don't
believe that all convictions are created equal, especially
when they come from a narrow, bigoted opinion.

—*Kim Campbell, March 10, 1988*

Kim Campbell was at the annual Canadian Bar Association
convention in Halifax in August of 1985, when the phone
rang in her hotel room. Bud Smith, the robust principal secretary
to Premier Bill Bennett, was calling from Victoria. Would she
come to work as the key policy adviser for the Tough Guy? It was
not the first time the two up-and-comers had spoken about her
political future under the Socreds. Bennett had had his eye on
Campbell ever since 1983, when she ran her no-holds-barred
campaign against the NDP in the provincial election.

In Bennett's mind, Kim Campbell, at 38, was the Grace
McCarthy of the 1980s. Like McCarthy, Campbell was an ambitious,

self-made woman with great potential. McCarthy had risen from near poverty to acquire both wealth and political power as a Socred minister. She now lived in the fashionable Shaughnessy district of Vancouver and wielded influence throughout the province. However, unlike the grandmotherly and ever-smiling McCarthy, the premier's new protégée had a razor-sharp mind and a knack for creating policy. "I brought her in for both policy development and policy analysis in my office," recalls Bennett. "She had opinions. She had an ability to do research. She wasn't someone to back down." Campbell jumped at the opportunity to join Bennett in his plans to promote free enterprise and give business access to British Columbia's vast resources. Young Bill was not a populist like his dad, W.A.C. "Wacky" Bennett, who had enjoyed a record-breaking 20 years in power during the boom times of the 1950s and 1960s. A calculating technocrat, Bill had recruited spin doctors from Ontario's famed Big Blue Machine to design policy from the pollsters' tea leaves. Campbell fitted comfortably into this team. Like Bennett, she tended to be anti-labor, disliking the unions for the Operation Solidarity walkouts of the early 1980s.

Although Campbell easily passed the premier's litmus test as a hard-line right-winger, Bennett's magicians did not have a confrontational mandate in mind for her. Because an election was just a year away, Socred strategists were determined to change the common perception that the premier was cold and bloodless. Campbell's task was to make Bennett's administration seem more human and lead the public to accept his dictum that economic development was the only social policy. Smith, now a businessman in his home town of Kamloops, B.C., remembers the rationale behind her job: "We had been through that really rigorous exercise of restraint and then the gameplan was to begin to develop new programs and new policies to . . . rebuild some processes for consensus within the province. There was a terrible amount of antagonism between various ideological groups and their decision makers."

Bennett announced Campbell's appointment as his executive director on August 29. In Victoria the next day, she was jubilant. "I think it's going to be challenging and interesting. I'll be working with Bud Smith and I have a lot of respect for him," she told reporters. "You will probably find me a little more reticent than before. I'm not going to shoot my mouth off like I did with the school board job. I'm working for somebody else now."

The move to Victoria was Campbell's next stepping-stone to political office. She had decided that practising law, like teaching college, was not the right career for her. Her ambitions were in the real world, where ideas could be put into action, says David Camp, a lawyer and son of famed Tory strategist Dalton Camp. Raised in the inner circle of the Tory party, Camp had been surrounded by politics since he was a baby bouncing on the knees of Richard Hatfield in New Brunswick. The two had met at Ladner Downs and would forge a close political alliance. "She decided this is what she wanted to do," says Camp. "She said she had a fascination for public policy and for communications and she felt that law was too narrow for her." The rising Socred star coyly deflected queries about seeking a seat in the legislature and a coveted cabinet post. "The job is not mutually exclusive of the other. Right now, I'm not thinking in those terms at all." Campbell did not fool anyone: she had been wearing her ambition on her sleeve ever since she had joined the Socreds in 1983.

The future looked rosy, and not just on the political front. At the annual meeting of the Canadian Bar Association, she had met Howard Eddy, a provincial government lawyer. Eddy, then 46, was a divorced father with three children. An American from Seattle and a former UBC law professor, the tall, lanky Eddy had handled most of B.C.'s unsuccessful cases involving aboriginal land claims. Campbell attracted him because, as he said, "She is vital, intelligent and compassionate."

At first Campbell was not charmed by Eddy, until a friend described the Abraham Lincoln lookalike as the "most brilliant and creative person" he knew. This was enough to make Campbell give him a closer look. "I'm a sucker for highly intelligent men," she said in a 1986 interview that took place one month before their wedding at the Vancouver Yacht Club.

In Campbell's eyes, Eddy was brilliant, fascinating and talented, a partner of whom she could be proud. He had attended Harvard University on a National Merit Scholarship, graduating *magna cum laude* in 1962. He started off in pre-med because he wanted to specialize in medical research. But midway through his undergraduate years he decided to become a lawyer. In addition to his intellectual credentials, Eddy was also a talented musician and a romantic outdoorsman who loved to sail and had once climbed Mt. St. Helens.

Like Campbell, Eddy shows a certain restlessness in both his career path and his family life. After serving three years as a naval officer in Vietnam, he and his wife, Sandra, left the United States and moved to Vancouver, where he enrolled in UBC's law school. He graduated with top marks and was hired as the law clerk of Chief Justice Robert Findley of the Washington State Supreme Court. In 1969 Eddy returned to Canada, where he taught law at UBC for two years before taking a leave of absence to work at the Law Reform Commission in Ottawa from 1972 until 1974.

Soon after he returned to teaching at UBC, Eddy quit his job and headed off to Queen's University to acquire the certification necessary to practise law in Ontario. In the late 1970s, he worked for both the Law Reform Commission and the Science Council and published two scholarly papers—one on automated banking and another on jurisdictional issues affecting the environment.

While they lived in Ontario, Howard and Sandra tried to resolve the difficulties in their marriage through counselling. However, the shy, withdrawn Eddy decided that the gulf between him and his outgoing wife was too wide to be bridged. One day in

1980, he suddenly announced to his family that he was taking his sailboat and returning to the West Coast.

Friends of Campbell's describe Eddy as very conservative and aloof. "He's cold, but she liked him a lot," recounts one close friend. Perhaps mindful of the happiness her mother had found in her second marriage, Campbell imitated Lissa and Bill's nautical lifestyle by moving aboard Eddy's 46-foot yacht, the *Western Yew*. On weekends, she and Howard sailed the Gulf Islands, listening to classical music and singing folk songs while he played the banjo and she the guitar. "They spent a lot of time on the *Western Yew*," says a friend. "When he met her he probably thought, at last, a woman who is willing to do what I want to do, which is to live aboard a boat and be somewhat of a nomad and cruise the islands and have somewhat of a laid-back life. He got more than he bargained for."

In her $45,000-a-year post, Campbell was part of an inner circle of top advisers who met the premier every morning to map out strategy and plan policy. She acted as liaison between Bennett and local Socred riding associations and co-ordinated the premier's public ventures outside Victoria. Her principal objective was to build bridges between the government and the anti-Socred coalition of unions, environmentalists, welfare advocates and still-bitter teachers. Invigorated by the challenge, she tackled the job with her usual high-octane energy. As soon as she moved into the Premier's Office she assembled the Wilderness Advisory Committee, made up of experts, businesspeople and environmentalists, to seek consensus about logging in B.C.'s provincial parks. She also sought to heal the wounds of the labor wars by meeting with teachers and unions to promote secondary education and job training. The Wilderness Committee later became the Commission on Resources and Environment, whose task was to come up with a province-wide plan to balance the objectives of maintaining jobs and preserving the environment.

All of Campbell's other initiatives were derailed on May 22, 1986, when Bennett announced that he was retiring from public life to return to the family business in Kelowna. Poll after poll had confirmed that the premier was extremely unpopular with the B.C. electorate after almost 11 tumultuous years in office.

Bennett's choice as his successor was Bud Smith, who had left as principal secretary a few months earlier to seek the nomination in the two-member riding of Kamloops. Smith, a bright, ambitious lawyer, had never held elective office, but neither had Bennett when he won the Socred leadership in November 1973. Passing the torch to the 40-year-old lawyer rankled cabinet veterans because they suspected that Smith had profited from advance knowledge of Bennett's plan to retire. Why else, they reasoned, would he embark on a province-wide tour to boost his image after winning the nomination? Socred veterans also believed Smith had got access to party membership lists in the Premier's Office.

The prospect of having a young pup like Smith capture the top prize was anathema to such party stalwarts as cabinet veteran Grace McCarthy, who had been in the legislature since 1966. "I don't believe in non-elected officials leading the province," she said. Credited with rebuilding the party after the NDP sweep of 1972, McCarthy, who felt the premiership was her due, was determined to stop the inexperienced Smith from grabbing the brass ring. Health Minister Jim Nielsen had similar feelings, which he expressed more bluntly. "I didn't shovel shit in the stables for ten years to have someone else come in and ride the pony," he declared.

Campbell's acquaintance with Smith had left her unimpressed with both his abilities and his Marlboro Man image. Appalled that he wore cowboy boots and checkered shirts to work, she considered herself brighter and more talented. "When it became clear he was going to be a candidate and a strong candidate," says David Camp, "she felt, if he's a strong candidate and I worked for him, I can compare myself to him. I know I have something to offer."

Camp warned Campbell that a leadership bid would be suicidal. She was, after all, a 39-year-old woman who had not accomplished much in her life and had lost her only bid for a seat in the legislature. How could she aspire to run the province?

Camp, who revered Campbell, did not wish to see her hurt. Over lunch at the Mandarin Hotel, he pleaded with her to abandon the pursuit of the premiership: "I remember making the case she shouldn't do it, that it might hurt her career, that she might not be able to run a credible campaign and she might not get an organization together or have enough money. I thought I had persuaded her not to run."

But Campbell did not heed Camp's advice. She was receiving encouragement from higher quarters. She was positive that she had a following in the party and that she could help the Socreds become a "really well established party, not dependent on one family." At the very least, a leadership bid would boost her popularity in the province. On June 12, she threw her hat into the ring, claiming she had received "enormous support and encouragement" from around the province. Campbell may have been known in Vancouver because of her three years on the school board, but the mass of Socred voters, let alone the rest of the province, had never heard of her. "She wasn't well known in the party," says Carol Gran, a friend who later served as caucus chair under Bill Vander Zalm. "She was known by the top brass, but the party's grass roots didn't know her."

Campbell's candidacy was a joke among the Socred hierarchy. Veteran cabinet minister Elwood Veitch remembers a conversation in Bennett's office after Campbell jumped into the race. "Is she for real?" one of Veitch's colleagues asked Bennett. "Oh yes," replied the premier. "She has stars in her eyes. I think she will come in dead bottom, but she still has stars in her eyes." Bennett did not tell Veitch that he had personally persuaded Campbell to seek the leadership in order to give the Socreds a more modern,

youthful image. "I actually encouraged her to seek it. I didn't necessarily expect her to win," says Bennett. "She spoke to a whole
group of people that I wanted to bring into politics and bring into
the party that may not have been there." Campbell did not see
herself as coming dead last. "I am in it to win," she told a CBC interviewer a few weeks before the convention.

Campbell garnered no corporate dollars and few supporters, although she was able to stake out some ground among reform-
minded members of the party. Just as she would do in her 1993 bid
for the leadership of the Conservative party, she talked about the
politics of inclusion and promised to be a conciliator, unlike her
old boss. She offered vague proposals about settling aboriginal
land claims, increasing educational spending and targeting welfare
to the truly needy. Even though her policies were insubstantial, at
least she put a few ideas before the voters, while her rivals tended
to spout rhetoric. One of her handful of supporters was Socred
Larry Pearce, a former law school chum. Pearce saw Campbell as a
viable candidate because "she has the ability to represent a broad
base of support without offending a lot of people."

No broad base of support materialized for her in the end. Too
many well-known Socreds, all vowing to end the years of confronta-
tion, had joined the contest and eclipsed Campbell's candidacy. By
mid-June, 11 contenders were in the running for the leadership of
their party. Among the heavyweight hopefuls were Bud Smith, Jim
Nielsen, Grace McCarthy, the party's conscience, and Stephen
Rogers, scion of the family that controlled B.C.'s sugar conglomer-
ate. Another important player was Brian Smith, the province's attorney general, who had the backing of the image makers of the Big
Blue Machine. Lesser lights were Bob Wenman, a Conservative MP
and a dour Bible thumper; Cliff Michael, a former mill worker; Bill
Ritchie, a born-again Christian MLA from the Fraser Valley; John
Reynolds, an MLA and former host of a radio talk show; and Mel
Couvelier, mayor of the Victoria suburb of Saanich.

The last to leap in was handsome Bill Vander Zalm, former Education minister, failed Vancouver mayoralty candidate and owner of the biblical theme park, Fantasy Garden World. Vander Zalm had been dithering as his phone line buzzed; the party faithful kept pleading with him to declare. He milked the publicity for all it was worth, hemming and hawing about running, largely out of concern for his shaky $7-million investment in Fantasy Gardens. He and his wife Lillian were immensely popular among Socreds because of their populism and staunch right-wing views. However, despite such strong support, Bennett and the party elite did not want Vander Zalm near the premier's chair. They considered the charismatic flower arranger to be an inept administrator and a renegade who would tear apart the party's delicate coalition of Liberals and Tories.

Vander Zalm had decided to join the race when he received a call from McCarthy, who feared the two Smiths might undo her hopes of becoming Queen of the Socreds. She reasoned that Vander Zalm's candidacy could rob delegates from Bud and Brian and allow her to have a clear run up the middle. "Grace phoned and said, 'Look, you have got to run. You are a good candidate and I think you should be in there with the rest of them running,'" Vander Zalm recalls. "And I had a long, long talk with Grace. And then Grace sort of convinced me that I should go in." When he declared himself a candidate on Friday, June 20, in the flower-bedecked atrium of Fantasy Gardens, he told the crowd, "I want to bring to government high moral standards based on true Christian principles."

Campbell had little respect for the Dutchman who had never attended university. Two reporters remember her saying, "I only wish I knew him before his lobotomy." What seemed to gall her most was Vander Zalm's ability to present himself as a man of the people even though he was a millionaire. She felt that her own humble origins deserved more attention. "Bill Vander Zalm likes to say he got his start at the end of a shovel," she asserted during the campaign. "Well, I got mine at the end of a halibut in Prince Rupert."

On July 28, 1986, more than 1,300 Socred delegates converged on the resort town of Whistler for only the second leadership convention in the 35-year history of their party. As is typical of political conventions, the crowd tended to be affluent and middle-aged, with the exception of several hundred youth delegates. In his book *Fantasy Government*, Stan Persky writes that half the delegates were 46 or older and most earned well over $50,000 a year. The majority had joined the party before 1975 and many were federal Tories.

By the time the charismatic Vander Zalm arrived at the three-day convention with Lillian and her colorful headbands, he had become the folk hero of the party and the darling of the media. A Vancouver *Sun* poll released two days before the convention showed him far ahead, with only Grace McCarthy coming anywhere near his popularity among delegates. He used no strategy other than shaking hands and flashing the megawatt smile that had become his trademark.

For Campbell, the bold challenge of trying for the leadership was becoming a nightmare. She had raised only $50,000 and, by the time the convention began, had barely enough money left to put up a small tent beside the giant ones of her opponents. The alpine town had become a glitzy, almost surreal Socred playground, swarming with men in white shoes and women in pastel pantsuits. A beaming Campbell would stand outside her tiny tent and wave to the crowd as they marched past her into the bigger tents where bands played late into the evening and the food and booze were free. All she could offer was soda pop and Rice Krispie squares in the shape of a K.

In bearpit sessions across the province, Campbell had failed to impress delegates as the self-described "candidate of ideas." Unable to strike a chord with the rank and file, she always came off as an elitist. "She had a tough time relating to a normal person," says Jim Nielsen, who remembers the discomfort Campbell felt at a country-and-western dinner for the candidates on Vancouver Island. "Well, Kim showed up in a cowgirl outfit, and she really didn't look comfortable. Kim looked like she had been decorated against her will." The novice politician was undoubtedly not used to such orchestrated events.

The impression that Campbell was out of touch with ordinary citizens had been reinforced in an interview she gave three weeks before the convention, at her home in Fairview Slopes. *The Vancouver Sun* was running a series on the 12 candidates and had assigned Gillian Shaw to write about Campbell. Perhaps because she was talking with a woman, Campbell felt at ease and opened up as she never had before, revealing the elitism that had begun to emerge in her years with Divinsky. "As an intellectually oriented person, I like to socialize with people who read the same things as I do"—Shaw wrote that she had mentioned Dostoyevsky, Tolstoy and Jane Austen—"and have a similar level of education, but I genuinely like ordinary people," she explained. "I think it's very important to realize that a lot of people that you are out there working for may sit in their underwear and watch the game on Saturday, beer in hand."

Shaw reported that Campbell said she did not want to socialize with such people: "I suppose they would find me as boring as I would find them." Nevertheless, she did want their support so that she could help them: "A lot of their attitudes you may not agree with, but they come from genuine human emotions—fear of change, fear of threat to their own security. If you don't understand that and like people, you can't deal with them, you can't take them anywhere."

When the article appeared in *The Vancouver Sun* on July 3, Campbell felt betrayed and claimed that Shaw had misrepresented what she had said. However, their conversation had been taped and the quotes were accurate. "That interview really traumatized Campbell," says *Sun* political columnist Vaughn Palmer, who remembers her being extremely thin-skinned in those days. "She talked about it years later. Her initial reaction was 'I couldn't have possibly said it.' But the fact is that nobody has actually challenged the quotes." Camp says the story "broke her heart" and "haunts her to this day." Campbell insisted that Shaw's portrait of her was unfair. "I detest intellectual pretension," she said. "I have a lot of faults but that ain't one of them." Diana Lam, her long-time friend and current aide in her riding association, believes the article derailed Campbell's bid for the leadership.

Shaw defends the article by pointing out that most of the text is in Campbell's own words. "She was upset by it and her campaign people called me," says the reporter. "There was not much I could do because this is what she said to me. I didn't describe her as arrogant. The conclusion was drawn by her own comments." Campbell says the incident taught her an important lesson: "That was the last time I was ever interviewed without taping the interview myself. That's why I am perhaps most comfortable on the radio or on television in a context that won't be edited. I'll take my lumps there."

One day before the leader was to be selected, delegates marched into the sweltering heat of the Whistler convention centre to hear five hours of oratory from the 12 candidates. Brian Smith arrived in the hall with a high-tech laser show featuring a green hand that reached out toward the slogan "The future that is ours to share." To the accompaniment of a disco tune, "Let Brian Take Us There," he stressed experience and ability in one of the best speeches of his life. Bud Smith sought to counter his lack of experience. "If elected experience was the only criterion, Dave Barrett would have made a hell of a premier," he said, referring to the NDP veteran and former B.C. premier. Grace McCarthy tried an appeal to the grass roots. "We do not reserve special places for the influential few; that is not my style," she said.

Campbell, the tenth speaker, was fortunate enough to hit a prime-time audience of several hundred thousand viewers.

Although she had scarcely enough supporters to carry her banner to the stage, witty remarks made her speech a success. "She came in with one piper [in a kilt]," says Camp, who was then working for Brian Smith. "She got up to the podium and got off five jokes that brought the house down." Delegates roared with laughter when Campbell quipped that she might have the smallest band in town but "mine's got better legs." Her self-deprecating humor contrasted sharply with the impression left by the Shaw piece a few weeks earlier. "You'll notice that my demonstration is simple this evening," she said. "Actually, I would have liked to have more but first of all none of my campaigners could do a hand-spring or a backflip. One of them volunteered to try but we couldn't afford the insurance premiums. We thought of trying to look like more people but none of them could run fast enough to get around to the end of the line in time."

In a substantive speech touching upon the two cornerstones of Socred ideology—individual freedom and free market dynamism— Campbell presented a more liberal vision to follow the Bennett years. Then she lambasted the premier's politics even though she had espoused them when she had chaired the school board, run for the legislature and served as one of Bennett's top aides. "I have a vision for this province," she said. "To succeed, we must rise above conflicts that divide us in education, in labor relations and in aboriginal claims. We must search for constructive poli-cies, for consensus and for the strengths that join the people of this province, not the weaknesses that divide."

She saw education as the key to prosperity. Big business, she said, should play a central role in reforming the system to ensure that displaced workers were retrained. In Campbell's world, indus-try would never lack a qualified labor supply. "It is time to stop thinking of education as a social service and to recognize it for what it is—an investment in human capital," she said. On the touchy issue of native land claims, Campbell tried to clear some ground to act as a social conciliator: "I have spoken about the need to build trust between our government and the native Indian community. . . . We can do so by showing our good will and willingness to work co-operatively with our native community." Then, assuring the delegates that she was "convinced of the correctness of our government's position," she repeated the Socred gospel on native land claims: British Columbia would refuse to negotiate claims until Ottawa agreed to pick up the multi-million-dollar tab.

The part of Campbell's speech in which she outlined her view of political leadership would reverberate longer and more ominously than any words spoken by any of the other contenders. "There are those who argue that all our problems result from a failure to make government simple," she said. "To be credible a leader must grasp the complex issues facing the government and avoid quick-fix solutions. The challenge of leadership is to build a talented team and to raise the level of public understanding. In this day and age, a leader cannot deceive the public with a simplistic vision of a past that can never be recaptured. Even the slickest salesmanship cannot sell for long a vision that is essentially empty, a vision that is really only a memory."

She paused to take a few jabs at the NDP opposition before delivering a devastating broadside against Vander Zalm. Without mentioning him by name, Campbell left no doubt that she believed the fantasy man could destroy the Social Credit Party. "It is fashionable to speak of leaders in terms of their charisma. But charisma without substance is a dangerous thing," she said to cheers and loud applause. "It raises expectations that cannot be satisfied. Then comes disillusionment and bitterness that destroys not only the leader but the party." Her speech so impressed the delegates that they rose to their feet as if they recognized the prophetic nature of her words without being able to heed her warning.

The last speaker was Vander Zalm. Rambling on for most of his speech, he produced only one memorable line. "This Bill needs your support on the first ballot," he said, in a reference to Bennett's first-ballot victory in 1973. "If I were choosing just from emotions and based on speeches, I'd choose Kim Campbell," Anne Paterson, a supporter of Brian Smith, told the *Sun*. "I was impressed by both Cliff Michael and Kim Campbell," said Vander Zalm enthusiast John Waterman. Richmond delegate Gerald Biggar also cast his vote for Vander Zalm but thought Campell was impressive. "I think she will become the sweetheart of the party," he predicted.

The next morning, delegates lined up at the voting booths as the Jazz Plus Trio played Duke Ellington's music in between floor demonstrations by the candidates' supporters. Shortly after noon, convention chair Les Peterson read the results of the first ballot. Vander Zalm had received 367 votes, well below the 648 needed to win. McCarthy was next with 244, followed by Bud Smith with 202, and Brian Smith with 196. There was a tie for fifth place between Jim Nielsen and John Reynolds, who each had 54 votes. Stephen Rogers was in seventh place with 43; and Wenman came in eighth with 40. Kim Campbell came in last with a humiliating total of 14 votes.

Campbell immediately walked to Brian Smith, the establishment's candidate of choice. Stephen Rogers, Bob Wenman and tenth-place finisher Bill Ritchie joined her in the trek. "Everyone is coming to us," exclaimed Patrick Kinsella, the field general of Smith's campaign. After the second ballot, Bud Smith, now in fourth place, joined Vander Zalm's camp, in hopes that he would be paid back with a cabinet slot. The vote came down to a final contest between Vander Zalm and Brian Smith. On the fourth ballot, the leadership was handed to Vander Zalm when McCarthy withdrew and most of her delegates went over to him. Vancouver *Sun* columnist Marjorie Nichols summed up the surprising outcome: "The neo-conservative Social Credit machine built by Bill Bennett is dead, the victim of a freakish head-on collision with a grassroots bulldozer driven by an unelected rampaging populist."

After the convention, Campbell returned to her home over-looking False Creek and the Vancouver skyline to lick her wounds. Worried about her state of mind after the disappointing last-place finish, David Camp took her to lunch. He told her that she was right in running for the leadership because the race had raised her profile across the province and among the party's grass roots. However, there was an important lesson for her to learn: put to-gether a machine of dedicated people before trying for a major political prize. Campbell's campaign had been a one-woman show; but successful politicians generally count on a team to tri-umph. "It's very hard for me to ask for help. It's something I have to overcome," she confessed. Camp understood at once that her upbringing had conditioned her to stand alone. "She was alluding to the circumstances in which she grew up where she was really required to take control of her life at an early age and be indepen-dent. That's always been her attitude."

One week after the convention, Vander Zalm was sworn in as British Columbia's twenty-seventh premier. He promised to run an open government that would consult widely and maintain high ethical standards. Despite her dislike of the new premier, Campbell decided to make a place for herself in the party led by the populist. She set her sights on winning a seat in the two-member riding of Vancouver–Point Grey, which had been held by cabinet members Pat McGeer and Garde Gardom, Liberals who were integral to the Socred coalition of Tories and Grits who had united to keep the NDP out of office. Gardom had stepped down to accept a sinecure as B.C.'s trade emissary in London.

Campbell pursued the nomination with her usual zeal. Again, she was the underdog facing an opponent's formidable organiza-tion. McGeer had decided that Dick Vogel, the former deputy at-torney general, would be an ideal candidate to replace Gardom. Anxious about Vander Zalm's ethics, McGeer felt there was a need to have an experienced legal mind at the cabinet table. "With

Vander Zalm having won the leadership, there was an urgent requirement for people with a strong legal background and considerable expertise in government," he recalled. Vogel had the backing
of the riding establishment, including Gardom, the riding president, and Robert Bonner, the former chairman of B.C. Hydro.

This time Campbell was ready to do battle. An enthusiastic
team of volunteers was recruited to conduct a phone blitz. She
also linked herself with the Socred infrastructure by seeking assistance from Bill Goldie, a prominent member of the Vancouver
Chamber of Commerce who had run Vander Zalm's leadership
campaign. McGeer's organizers had not realized that Goldie lived
in the riding. He was flattered when Campbell, who had spotted
his name on the party's membership lists, asked for help in bringing out the grass-roots vote. Her fight for the nomination would
have been closer had Vogel not shot himself in the foot a few
days before the vote by admitting to reporters that he was not a
member of the party. Campbell won the nomination 176 to 129
and went on to win the seat for the Socreds in the October 22
provincial election, where she topped the polls with 17,596
votes. McGeer lost his seat to New Democrat Darlene Marzari.

In the victory speech she delivered at Socred headquarters on
West 10th Avenue, Campbell had little to say about what her goals
would be in the legislature. She also refused to speculate on whether
she would get a cabinet slot. "Mostly what I'm interested in providing is a conciliatory atmosphere," she stated. The election had
been a massive rout of the socialists: the Socreds captured 47 seats
while the NDP held only 22. Vander Zalm was overwhelmed by his
victory. "My office is going to play a stronger role in the governing
of the province," he declared. For many in British Columbia his
words would prove all too true.

Clearly, Campbell expected to be appointed to the cabinet
since she had better credentials than many of the Socred MLAs
and had run for the leadership. But, on November 6, when

Vander Zalm unveiled his first cabinet, Campbell and Bud Smith were not among the chosen. At Whistler, both leadership contenders had distanced themselves from the premier's right-wing version of Christian morality; and even though Smith had scurried over to Vander Zalm's box at the very end, he was still out of favor. The premier selected Brian Smith and Grace McCarthy, who had been members of Bennett's cabinet, and five rookies, including Mel Couvelier, who was his surprise choice for Finance minister. He distributed the rest of the portfolios to loyal followers and ideological soulmates.

There could be little doubt that Vander Zalm was angry at Campbell for her "charisma without substance" speech. He also was not inclined to appreciate the talents of an urbane intellectual with liberal sympathies. Yet he insists that he did not exclude Campbell from his cabinet out of any dislike for her personally or because of an urge for revenge. "The choice of the first cabinet was made on the basis of experience—also taking into consideration geography and who could serve best in what position and those sorts of things. So there was nothing magical about it," Vander Zalm explains. "It wasn't personal. I had a number of liberal people in the cabinet. She didn't make it because the chips fell that way."

Campbell was one of nine women elected to the B.C. legislature in 1986. Since 1918 the province had elected only 33 women to serve as members of the legislature, a mere seven of whom had been appointed to cabinet. Although British Columbia was thus no haven for female politicians, it was historically known to be a place where women could be promoted to high office. In 1921, Mary Ellen Smith had been appointed the first woman cabinet minister in the British Empire.

When Campbell took up the duties of a backbench MLA, she was one of only four women in a Socred caucus largely composed of men who believed that women should stay away from the business of government. "It was a sexist caucus," says Carol Gran, who was elected in the Vander Zalm sweep and became Campbell's roommate and confidante. "There was a fair amount of male chauvinism in that caucus room and they had no time for daycare or concerns about violence against women," she remembers.

Campbell's seatmate was her former boss, Bud Smith. He speaks of her approvingly as an MLA who cared passionately about "restraint and fiscal responsibility." However, she alienated many of her male colleagues from the day she set foot in the legislature because she was far too outspoken and self-confident. Determined to make an impression and to influence policy making, she was not afraid to challenge cabinet ministers, who quickly learned to come prepared for any caucus meeting in which they had to explain planned legislation. "She wanted to know all the facts and all the reasons for a decision," recalls Elwood Veitch, who was then provincial secretary and not one of Campbell's fans. "She didn't always buy the program. She was very analytical and a little stand-offish. I had to spend a lot time preparing if I knew Kim was in caucus."

Campbell had just turned 40 when she took her seat in Victoria's impressive chamber, with its plush red carpet and dark marble walls. "I am overcome by the sense of awe at the opportunity to speak in this chamber," she said in a reply to the Throne Speech on March 16. Her maiden speech dealt largely with her interest in improving education and the proposed $2 billion KAON particle physics project slated for UBC, which was in her riding. In the 128 speeches she delivered in the legislature that year, she would show herself to be a small "c" conservative and an enthusiastic supporter of most of the government's far-right legislative initiatives.

Social activists were alarmed when the government proposed changes to the province's health statutes. One new amendment would give health officers the power to quarantine people with communicable diseases. Although the change was aimed at controlling tuberculosis patients who acted irresponsibly by exposing other people to the disease, the amendment raised fears because of Vander Zalm's anti-gay ravings and Health Minister Peter Dueck's public musings about mandatory AIDS testing. While Campbell did use her influence on behalf of the B.C. Civil Liberties Association to water down the statute and guarantee due process, in a speech to the legislature in November 1987, she denied that AIDS was a serious disease. "It is a great pity that there is an overfixation on AIDS, which is perhaps one of the least concerns in our society right now with respect to infectious or contagious diseases," she said. "I don't think AIDS is a particularly contagious disease."

Campbell was appointed to the Health, Education and Social Services Committee and later chaired both the Select Standing Committee on Labour, Justice and Intergovernmental Relations and the Project Pride task force, whose report laid the foundation for B.C.'s policy on heritage conservation. However, she soon discovered that legislative committees had little clout because Vander Zalm had centralized power in his office by having deputy ministers report directly to him or his top aides. Nevertheless, although she did not have much influence on policy, she did enjoy the thrust and parry of parliamentary debates in which NDP members felt the sting of her remarks. "The honorable member's intellectual condescension is often very hard to take," she told one NDP MLA who had laughed at her for saying that she had been reading the diaries of British cabinet minister Richard Crossman. "I do have an I.Q. in three digits," she told him. "It may surprise him to know that I do read those diaries without moving my lips and I am able to understand them. I don't even run my finger along the lines as I read them."

Another time she silenced a noisy heckler by asking, "Are words of two syllables a little difficult for you to understand?" Then she added, "I hope those scabs on your knuckles aren't distressing you too much." New Democrat Moe Sihota, now a cabinet minister under Mike Harcourt, acknowledges that Campbell is a skilled communicator in debate but believes that her competence hides contempt for others. "Underneath that veneer lies someone who is arrogant, self-righteous and very much [certain that] her view is the exclusive view," he says.

The policy to which Campbell gave her most outspoken support was Vander Zalm's decision to drastically rewrite the labor laws. The progressive 1973 Labour Code was to be wiped out by his hastily written Bill 19, which appointed a new labor czar who would wield massive powers to intervene and halt disputes that threatened the public interest. A companion piece of legislation, Bill 20, gave teachers the right to strike but also allowed teachers in each district to vote on whether they wanted a union. In an attempt to further weaken the teachers' federation, control of certification and disciplining of teachers was to be assumed by a new College of Teachers. Drafted by Vander Zalm's office without consultation with senior bureaucrats in the labor department, these changes amounted to a frontal assault on B.C.'s trade unionists.

Campbell praised the changes as "new and innovative" and denounced the labor movement's mounting campaign to kill the legislation. "I think we have to be honest about why these amendments are before this House, why they are required," she told the legislature on April 14. "They are required because there are many people in our society who regard unions as unfair and who feel there should be more government control over them." It was a startling statement from a woman who believed in making government smaller and less intrusive. Two days later, Campbell continued this rhetoric, insisting that there was "widespread public disenchantment with organized labor" and that it was necessary to rein in radical labor leaders who learned "their social attitudes in Liverpool and Manchester and on the Clydeside."

Many British Columbians disagreed with Campbell about the merits of busting unions. Even the Business Council of B.C.

complained that the bill had removed the incentive to compromise during negotiations. In June, 300,000 unionists launched a one-day general strike that stopped buses and ferries, closed schools and hospitals and even halted garbage pick-up. Polls showing the Socreds only nine points behind the NDP opposition revealed that a whopping 50 percent of the electorate believed Bill 19 was unfair and that 44 percent endorsed the illegal strike. The unpopularity of this policy—one of the few on which Campbell and the premier saw eye to eye—marked the beginning of the end for Vander Zalm.

Campbell's first major clash with the premier during her term as an MLA occurred in June 1987, when the Social Credit caucus announced plans to hold a two-day retreat at Fantasy Gardens. The New Democrats loudly protested the petty greed displayed by this obvious conflict of interest. Unfazed by the criticism, the premier defended the party's payments to Fantasy Gardens, claiming that the rent was cheaper than "we could possibly get anywhere." Besides, Vander Zalm said he could "invite to my place whomever it is I please."

Campbell was outraged that the premier would profit from a party function and sent off a personal letter scolding him for his lack of ethics. Vander Zalm's office leaked the letter to the media with the mistaken belief that it would discredit Campbell. It had the opposite effect: the letter demonstrated to British Columbians that Campbell was gutsy and had the principles that their premier lacked. It was the beginning of an even greater fight.

Bill and Lillian Vander Zalm were tanning themselves on the beaches of Hawaii when the Supreme Court of Canada rendered a judgment that would change Campbell's life. On January 28, 1988, in a five to two decision, the high court threw out Canada's abortion law that declared it unconstitutional to require a woman to get the approval of a hospital's therapeutic abortion committee in order to have an abortion. "Forcing a woman, by threat of criminal sanction, to carry a fetus to term unless she meets certain criteria

unrelated to her own priorities and aspirations, is a profound interference with a woman's body and thus an infringement of security of
the person," Chief Justice Brian Dickson wrote in his majority ruling.
Justice Bertha Wilson, the first woman appointed to the Supreme
Court, said that an abortion was "essentially a moral decision and in
a free democratic society the conscience of the individual must be
paramount to that of the state."

The premier and his wife were shocked and enraged. Bill Vander
Zalm concurred with Lillian, a devout Roman Catholic, that abortion was a sin. The next day he phoned Health Minister Dueck, a
zealous pro-lifer, to discuss the government's response to the court's
judgment. Without approval from cabinet or caucus, the two decided
that despite the high court's ruling, the provincial government
would pay only for abortions approved by a hospital's therapeutic
abortion committee. "We do not believe that taxpayers' dollars
should be used to fund abortion on demand," Dueck said. "We believe an abortion to be funded by the taxpayer should be medically
required."

Nine days after the Supreme Court's judgment, Vander Zalm
upped the ante when he and Lillian landed at Vancouver airport
sporting dark tans. "I will recommend to cabinet tomorrow that
the government no longer pay for any abortions, save those in
emergency situations," he declared. "I want to free taxpayers
from abortions. . . . Abortions diminish a society's respect for human rights." A day later, Vander Zalm said his new policy would
also apply to victims of rape and incest. The B.C. Medical
Association was swift in announcing its refusal to go along with
his policy. The Vancouver *Province* called the premier's stance an
"outrageous response to a decision of Canada's highest court."
Critics noted wryly that while Vander Zalm voiced deep concern
for the fetus, his own policies showed a heartless disregard for
the well-being of single mothers and needy families. He had refused to pay for school lunches for undernourished children on

the grounds that their parents' welfare cheques were being wasted on other things.

When the Socred caucus met to discuss the controversial abortion policy, MLA Russ Fraser was the only one to ask Vander Zalm for an explanation. Campbell kept quiet even when the premier asked if there were any questions or concerns. "We opened the meeting with that. Everybody had an opportunity to speak out on the issue," Vander Zalm told journalists Gary Mason and Keith Baldrey. "A few people did. A very few. And those that did speak out were largely on the supportive side. I guess I was impressed by the solidarity of the caucus at that time."

When Campbell arrived at her office after the caucus meeting, she was surprised to find an enormous pile of telephone messages from outraged constituents in her prosperous riding. The calls were running four to one against the government. She was pro-choice, but had maintained her silence, hoping she could privately use moral suasion to change Vander Zalm's mind. On February 11, after a hostile meeting with Dueck, she had harsh criticism for Vander Zalm. "It would be hypocritical to suggest I support the policy," she told CBC TV. "My pro-choice views are well known." Campbell asserted that it was wrong for the government to renege on its obligation to fund medical services in order to impose a moral standard that was not shared by the populace as a whole. "I think it's wrong in law. It offended my principles of freedom of religion and freedom of conscience."

The next day three more MLAs split with Vander Zalm. Caucus chair Carol Gran made the move despite concern that she might jeopardize her chances for re-election in the largely rural riding of Langley. Although three others, including Socred matriarch Grace McCarthy, also broke ranks with the premier over the next week, none was as outspoken as Campbell. Gran said she backed the "premier all the way" except for the rape and incest provisions. David Poole, the premier's top aide, made a point of telling reporters that

Vander Zalm had the support of the entire caucus except for Campbell. Still, Campbell did not back off. "Our party is not a pro-life party," she said as the dispute garnered front-page headlines. "We come together because we share certain views on the relationship between governments and the economy and the individual in society. We don't come together on the issue of abortion, which cuts across parties." Later she told *The Globe and Mail* columnist Stevie Cameron that Vander Zalm's anti-abortion stance had "come from a narrow, bigoted opinion."

Campbell's fate within the Socred party seemed to be sealed. Her comment at the convention about charisma without substance and her letter decrying the caucus meeting at Fantasy Gardens had enraged the premier. Her vocal opposition to his abortion policy was the last straw. "Campbell was a backbencher with a man who was very much in power in a party that had never tolerated dissent. It was a career-limiting move," recalls Vaughn Palmer. Campbell did not improve her relationship with the premier when she performed a humorous skit mocking his eccentricities at the 1988 Victoria press gallery party. "It was very funny," says Gran. "The reporters then started singing 'Bye, Bye Kim.'"

However, despite Vander Zalm's antipathy, Campbell was riding a wave of public approval. A Socred poll released in the midst of the controversy about abortion revealed that 60 percent of British Columbians backed Campbell's pro-choice position. Vander Zalm was saved from further backlash on March 7 when the B.C. Supreme Court ended the brouhaha by ruling that the premier had gone beyond "common sense" in cutting off abortion funding. Believing that Campbell had turned the caucus against him, Vander Zalm never forgave her for her public criticism. "She sort of went out to the media and that was the beginning of a bit of a breakdown because others followed," he said. "I guess she wasn't the only one of that mind, but the others sort of kept it to themselves in caucus."

The argument about abortion eventually faded away as other contentious issues rose to claim public attention in the crisis-filled months that followed. The government had decided to sell some prized real estate—50 square blocks of land that had been the site of Expo 86. One of Vander Zalm's cronies, millionaire business-man Peter Toigo, offered $500 million to buy the property. Grace McCarthy was shocked at the special treatment afforded Toigo. She believed that Vander Zalm and David Poole had given him confidential information about the bidding. She resigned in protest on July 5, 1988, one day before the premier shuffled his cabinet, naming Bud Smith as his attorney general and promoting eight backbenchers. Vander Zalm's new cabinet looked lopsided: there was no one at the table from Vancouver and only one woman, Municipal Affairs Minister Rita Johnston.

Once again the talents of Gran and Campbell were ignored. When a reporter asked the premier why he had only one woman in his cabinet, Vander Zalm snapped, "Oh, my goodness, I don't think the women of the province are as picky as you." Campbell complained bitterly that the premier had excluded MLAs from the biggest city in the province while giving representation to ar-eas with only a quarter of the population. Vander Zalm says that Campbell was lobbying for the attorney general's job at the same time that she was plotting against him with caucus colleagues. "She certainly, I think, sought a particular position which was shuffled a number of times, namely the attorney general's position," he recalls. He says that he refused to promote her because "she was very opinionated and she wanted her own way."

In August, Vander Zalm, tarnished by scandal and crippled by infighting, summoned his caucus to a retreat in Courtenay, a scenic resort north of Victoria. He faced a revolt over the general incompetence of his government and the impropriety of his deal with Toigo. Polls indicated that the premier's approval rating had dipped to 19 percent. Donations to the Socreds had plummeted,

and membership in the party was declining. In an effort to heal
the growing rift between the caucus and the Premier's Office,
David Poole resigned. Most Socreds were convinced that Vander
Zalm had to follow him. Former cabinet minister Russ Fraser led
a group of eight backbenchers who planned to call for a secret
leadership vote at the fall convention. Campbell joined the plot,
along with Gran, McCarthy and Brian Smith.

When the caucus met, Campbell and backbench MLA Norm
Jacobsen were brutally honest in their assessment of Vander
Zalm's leadership. Jacobsen told the premier that the Socreds
were doomed unless he altered his behavior radically. Campbell
said Vander Zalm had the potential to be a good leader and that
he should take the harsh criticism as a "learning experience."
Several caucus members were so impressed by Campbell's performance that they later told a reporter from B.C. *Politics and Policy*
that she possessed "largely male attributes." In an effort to repair
his tattered reputation, Vander Zalm conceded that he had made
mistakes and promised to consult his caucus and inner cabinet on
all issues in the future. "You will see more unity in caucus and my
personal feeling is you will see very little dissent," Gran predicted
to reporters at the end of the meeting.

Nothing could have been further from the truth. The eight dissidents proceeded with their plans for a secret ballot at the October
1988 convention in Penticton. Campbell's riding president, Alistair
Palmer, joined other Vancouver riding executives in the scheme.

All of a sudden, Campbell backed out of the coup. She was
rapidly losing interest in her legislative duties and had not even
bothered to show up to vote for the Meech Lake Accord when it
came before the legislature. Her eyes were now turning eastward to
Ottawa, where she felt her ambitions could be realized under a different leader—one who would appreciate her talents.

In her two years as MLA, Campbell had developed a political
style that reflected her beliefs and personality: she was combative

and unafraid to speak out on controversial issues; she played the game by men's rules; she showed a politician's instinct for adapting her principles when expedient; and she was unashamedly ambitious.

5

POWERTOWN

> This is a game in which women have very little power. . . .
> You can address it by going along with the agenda of those
> in power who can help you or you can address it by taking
> your own agenda and fighting every step of the way.
>
> —*Mary Clancy,*
> *Liberal MP*

In August 1988, Prime Minister Brian Mulroney, rebounding from scandals that besmirched the early Tory years, was poised to call an election. The Conservative government's attempt to push the Canada–United States free trade deal through Parliament had been blocked by Liberal senators led by wily Allan MacEachen, the masterful parliamentary tactician who had engineered the downfall of the Clark government in 1980. Prospects of winning a second majority mandate were promising now that John Turner's competence had been tarnished by a series of caucus revolts over his stewardship of the once great Liberal party. Sitting nine points ahead of the Grits in the polls, the Tories had a political machine that was well oiled and ready for battle.

Conservative strategists were worried about support in British Columbia, where anti-free trade sentiment was running high. West Coast voters had grown disillusioned with Mulroney, partly because of their unhappiness with the Socreds, his Tory cousins in Victoria. The exuberant New Democrats aspired to capture between 11 and 16 of the province's 32 federal seats. Mulroney was troubled by the lack of high-profile candidates in the province. Of the three cabinet ministers from B.C., only Treasury Board president Pat Carney had any stature; most of the backbench MPs were considered right-wing lightweights. Although John Fraser was well liked, the Speaker of the House of Commons had made the wise decision to campaign as an independent in his riding of Vancouver South.

Campbell was an ideal candidate for the Tories: she was bright, attractive and distanced from the floundering Vander Zalm regime. In the summer months, she had been approached to run for the nomination in John Turner's riding of Vancouver Quadra. However, at that time she decided not to disrupt her life by going after a job that would require a move to faraway Ottawa. She and her husband loved to spend their weekends sailing the *Western Yew*, which they moored at a Sidney marina. They also enjoyed the evenings they spent in Vancouver attending concerts and the theatre or entertaining at Campbell's home in Fairview Slopes.

Furthermore, Campbell did not relish the thought of waging a battle against the Liberal leader after fighting a hard election contest only two years before. And she may have harbored hopes that Vander Zalm would promote her to cabinet. "I kept saying no, no, that I have made my commitment provincially," she explained to B.C. *Politics and Policy*. "I told all these people, 'Keep looking for other candidates, it's unlikely that I will make the move.'"

Toward the end of August, Pat Carney, the architect of the free trade agreement, began to have second thoughts about seeking

another term. Plagued by arthritis, she concluded that she did not
have the stamina to run a 51-day campaign in Vancouver Centre,
a horseshoe-shaped riding stretching from the established, wealthy
region of Point Grey to the trendier neighborhood of Kitsilano,
with its diverse population of gays, senior citizens and young professionals. The riding is a significant one; traditionally it has produced many cabinet ministers. Now, internal Tory polls revealed
Carney to be ten points behind her rival, Johanna den Hertog,
the national president of the NDP, who had lost to the minister by
4,800 votes in 1984.

Carney and her campaign boss, Lyall Knott, looked upon
Campbell as an ideal candidate to bear the Tory flag since the
riding encompassed part of her own provincial district. "She was
the first person I called," says Carney. But Campbell rebuffed the
Tory invitation once again. "I was at the time touring with one of
my legislative standing committees and I just felt I have a commitment; there were things I wanted to do here. I wasn't eager for
another campaign," she explained. Knott says that when the offer
was made, Campbell told him it was too complicated at the time
to make a career change. "She had a husband who had a job in
Victoria. She had a place and their life was nice. She was a
Socred backbencher, very frustrated, but to go to Ottawa, 2,500
to 3,000 miles away, is a whole change in life and career."

The search for another name candidate began in earnest. Rick
Hansen, who had won the hearts of Canadians with his round-the-
world trek in a wheelchair, was approached, as was his father-in-
law, Patrick Reid, the former head of Expo 86. *The Vancouver Sun*
columnist Nicole Parton and gruff BCTV talk show host Jack
Webster were also wooed. All four declined. When the hugely popular Webster turned them down, the Tories anxiously sought out
Campbell once again. On October 9, Carney telephoned her and
got a different response: Campbell now expressed more interest in
accepting the federal nomination. She had begun to reconsider her

decision to stay out of federal politics after attending a convention of the Union of British Columbia Municipalities, in Whistler, where Turner was the keynote speaker. "I heard him completely distort the free trade agreement and say things that I think were misleading," Campbell told Gary Mason of *The Vancouver Sun* a few weeks later. "It really kind of frightened me. . . . I think it's unbelievably damaging and hurts the integrity of the political process."

A second factor that influenced her to run federally was the encouragement she received from Howard Eddy, who by now had agreed to pull up stakes and move to the nation's capital if the election turned in her favor. "He'd always said he was 50/50 about it—because he can relocate and go to Ottawa—and it was really my decision," Campbell said. "And finally I said, 'Howard, it can't just be my decision.' And he said, 'Go for it.'"

There was a third reason for Campbell to run. Although she was 15 points behind den Hertog, she thought the tide was turning. The great TV showdown on October 25, 1988, in which John Turner would triumph over Brian Mulroney on the issue of free trade, had not yet occurred, and Knott remembers that "it looked like the Conservatives were going to win the election at that point."

Campbell flew to Victoria to inform Vander Zalm of her decision to resign from the legislature should she win the federal riding. The premier described Campbell as a "very bright individual" and predicted she would get the seat. Privately he was dismayed, not because he would miss the outspoken rebel, but because her resignation would trigger a by-election that the Socreds were sure to lose. For her part, Campbell insisted that she was not leaving out of bitterness. "You don't run for office to escape from something," she told Mason. "If I were really unhappy provincially and didn't want to serve anymore, then I could just resign, go back and practise law or something." However, two months later, Campbell admitted to Steve Mertl of Canadian Press that she might not have run federally if Vander Zalm had elevated her from the backbenches to the cabinet table. "I didn't get the opportunity to do a lot of things I wanted to get done," she said. "That wasn't my choice. For some reason the premier didn't want to put me in cabinet. A lot of my colleagues wanted to see me there." Carol Gran saw pure ambition behind Campbell's move to the federal Tories. "She did what was best for Kim."

Campbell launched her campaign once again as an underdog. The election race had officially begun two weeks before her October 18 nomination meeting, but den Hertog, a soft-spoken 36-year-old who looks a bit like Mila Mulroney, had been knocking on doors since the summer. She had assiduously courted the large gay vote by pledging both to fight for more money for AIDS research and to press for more experimental drugs to be made available to patients with the deadly disease. Ed Broadbent's vow to change the Canadian Human Rights Act to end discrimination based on sexual orientation made den Hertog a popular candidate for the NDP.

Campbell's Liberal rival was 48-year-old Tex Enemark, a mining executive and one-time aide to former Trudeau cabinet minister Ron Basford, who had held the riding in the late 1970s. Enemark was basing his campaign on support for Turner's angry opposition to free trade, but stood little chance of winning because so few voters in the riding knew either his history or his name.

About 400 of the Tory faithful and 12 MPs turned out for Campbell's nomination meeting in a hall on West 4th Avenue. Pat Carney had removed her high heels to relieve the pain of her arthritis. Standing at the podium in her stocking feet, she praised her successor as a "rising star." Campbell won by acclamation, the only dissent coming from a woman at the back of the hall who complained that a formal yea or nay was needed to finalize the selection. The dissident got her way and journalist Mark Hume reported that "the yeas just about blew the doors off the packed meeting. . . . Only two nays were raised against Campbell, while about 400 cheered and clapped to confirm her."

In her acceptance speech, Campbell unleashed a scathing attack on Turner and Broadbent. The crowd was delighted with the new Tory dynamo's aggressive approach to partisan politics and relished the prospect of watching her perform on the hustings. "Canadians must reject the appeals of those political leaders Jingo John and Oshawa Ed, who wrap themselves in the flag while they not only sell Canadians short but sell them out," she thundered. She described Broadbent as a malevolent socialist and a hypocrite to boot, who "warns us of the evils of American investment and American multinationals, but . . . loves General Motors, which has invested $8 billion in his riding." It was a barnburner of a speech that she would use to great effect throughout her campaign.

Support for the free trade deal had slipped badly after Mulroney lost the TV debate in a toe-to-toe exchange with Turner. By early November, with 55 percent of B.C. voters against free trade (compared with 23 percent in favor), Campbell was also drawing negative press coverage for her often nasty putdowns of those who opposed the deal. At an all-candidates debate in a West End community centre, she screamed at hecklers in the audience, "What are you afraid of?" Enemark was stunned at her outburst. "She was on the edge of tears the whole time," he told reporters after the heated debate. "She gets very emotional. She kind of loses her grip on things."

Campbell did not recount the incident in the same terms. Although she admitted that she had lost her cool, she insisted that she had made the only intelligent remarks of the evening. "I have had so many people come and say 'You were the only rational person there,'" she said. "When people hear intelligent reasonable discussion of the free trade agreement from someone who understands what it's all about, they respond."

Her attacks turned Enemark and den Hertog into bitter foes. It was one thing to be engaged in a spirited battle; it was quite another to be treated with contempt. "Kim is very much above the rest of us," Enemark remarked at the time. "She has a firm grasp of the truth, that's the impression she gives. Everyone else is either stupid or a liar." Den Hertog described Campbell as "loud, aggressive and accusatory."

Although her approach was heavy-handed, few impartial observers could deny that Campbell's arguments had merit. Having carefully read the free trade pact, including the fine print, she found it maddening to listen to anti-free traders misrepresent the text of the accord in order to accuse the Tories of selling Canada out to American multinationals. She regarded the charge that the agreement would dismantle cherished Canadian social programs as false and considered her support for free trade to be based on factual and objective criteria. When she thought her opponents lied about the substance of the deal, she retaliated with caustic sarcasm.

Her impassioned defence of the accord and her stinging criticism of its detractors made Campbell B.C.'s best-known crusader for free trade. Nevertheless, although her reasoning could be convincing, many voters were hostile to the style in which she presented her arguments. Knott says that as the election drew closer, the Tory brain trust in Ottawa became increasingly sure that she could not win the race. In a desperate attempt to muster support for the deal, major corporations financed last-minute television advertisements endorsing the Tories. However, internal party polls revealed that Campbell was going to lose to den Hertog despite this last-minute support.

Flushed and feverish, Campbell was suffering from a cold on the day of the November 21 election. But illness did not dampen her resolve to try everything possible to snatch victory from the jaws of defeat. She and Knott assembled a team of 600 members to get out the vote. They made sure that anyone who had ever uttered a good word about the Tories was transported to the polling booths.

Not long after the polls closed in Ontario and Quebec, CBC anchor Peter Mansbridge declared that Mulroney had won a second majority government—the first time a Tory leader had accomplished this feat since Sir John A. Macdonald's victory in 1891. Many hours would pass before Campbell could know her fate. In B.C. the New Democrats were bucking the Conservative tide that was washing over most of the land by leading in 19 of the 32 electoral races. Campbell went home to sleep before the verdict for Vancouver Centre was announced early the next morning. At 4 A.M., a reporter called to inform the new MP of her 279-vote victory over den Hertog. She had received 23,532 votes to den Hertog's 23,253, while Enemark had finished a distant third with just over 14,000. "What a landslide," quipped Campbell when she heard the final tally. (A recount reduced her margin by 10 votes.)

The results of the 1988 election did not pose a significant challenge to patriarchy in Ottawa, where Campbell would soon go: only 40 of the 295 elected MPs were women. However, even though Parliament remained very much a male enclave, for the first time since Confederation, female MPs came together in a sustained effort to combat sexism in the institution. New Democrats Dawn Black and Lynn Hunter, Liberal Mary Clancy and Conservative Barbara Greene joined with other colleagues, including three cabinet ministers—Mary Collins, Monique Landry and Barbara McDougall—to form the Women's Parliamentary Association, a group devoted to improving conditions for all women who worked on the Hill. When Deborah Grey of the Reform Party joined the association in 1991 after winning a by-election, the group could claim members from four national parties.

The association convinced the Speaker to hire sexual harassment officers to deal with women's complaints about the improper behavior of some male bosses. Since, unlike other workplaces, Parliament is exempt from the Canadian Human Rights

Act, employees on the Hill have no collective rights and can be fired without cause. Female workers are thus entirely dependent on the good will of male supervisors. As well as giving women some means to counter harassment, the group tried to improve working hours for female MPs with young children and to provide safer conditions for all women who work at night.

Feminist MPs also acted individually to challenge a range of sexist practices, customs and conditions. Several complained about internal memos that routinely addressed them as "Mr." and a few rejected lapel pins that were designed for male clothing. New Democrat Joy Langan walked into the male MPs' gym in the Confederation Building and started to work out in surroundings that were far better outfitted than the room for women one floor up. Greene demanded better lighting and patrolling in the parking lots after she was assaulted in a dark area. As a rule, such feminist activity on the Hill was concerned with issues of equity and safety rather than with partisanship or ideology.

Although Kim Campbell says she is a feminist, she did not take part in these efforts to counter sexism in Parliament. Dawn Black recalls Campbell's absence from the group: "We worked on making structural changes in this place but she never joined in the meetings; I saw no effort on Kim's behalf to make institutional change in this place." Besides her lack of interest in working with feminist MPs, Campbell's attitude irked several female colleagues who found her cold and aloof.

Clancy remembers an encounter at CTV's Ottawa bureau when she, Black and Campbell were being interviewed on "Canada AM" as up-and-coming women politicians. Before the show, Campbell was sitting in the lounge reading *The Globe and Mail* when Clancy arrived and Black introduced them. "Well, I'm Kim Campbell and I'm a lawyer," she snapped to the startled Clancy. "I thought she was a real snot," recalls Clancy. "I said, 'I'm a lawyer too.'" "She seems so incapable of warmth despite her occasional sense of humor," says Black. "You know, there are only 40 of us and we have things in common regardless of our political affiliation. There is not an element of interest or friendship from her."

Other feminists of the left charge that Campbell talked the talk but never walked the walk. To them, her feminism has less to do with promoting equality of rights and opportunity than with ensuring positions of power to professional women. Vancouver feminist Shelagh Day, vice-president of the National Action Committee on the Status of Women (NAC), says Campbell did not support the feminist movement in B.C. Although feminists were delighted with her pro-choice stance against Vander Zalm, they saw little evidence that she cared about promoting their agenda. "She is interested in women like herself having positions of power," Day explains. "That's not what being a feminist means to me. What being a feminist means to me is that you, in fact, are interested in the equality of all women and you are interested in the advancement of women, particularly the most disadvantaged women."

However, there is another point of view on the opinion that Campbell is not the right kind of feminist. Kathleen Mahoney, a feminist law professor at the University of Calgary, says Campbell practises a feminism that differs from the mainstream women's movement. "When she says she's a feminist, I really think she is genuine; she understands how women have been discriminated against."

Ottawa lawyer Jennifer Lynch, national president of the Progressive Conservative Women's Federation, also believes that Campbell is committed to the advancement of women, particularly in politics. She dismisses criticism from NAC as left-wing polemics: "Kim Campbell's value system is very definitely to encourage the equality of each Canadian. NAC's leadership takes partisan views on just about every topic and is anti-everything. It doesn't surprise me since they are anti-everything our government does that they would be anti-Kim Campbell."

Campbell bristles when women like Judy Rebick, the past president of NAC, suggest that she is not a feminist. She believes that
feminists of the left smear her as an anti-feminist because she is a
fiscal conservative. "I see nothing inconsistent with my deep
commitment to feminism and my deep commitment to fiscal ra-
tionality and to sound economic policy," she says. "That to me is
the guarantee of the type of thing I want to accomplish for women
in this country."

When Campbell arrived in Ottawa, there was little doubt in
her mind that Brian Mulroney would bring her into the inner
sanctum of power. During campaign appearances on the West
Coast, she had impressed both the prime minister and Mila
Mulroney with her encyclopedic knowledge of the free trade
agreement. Mulroney loves politicians with guts and he was awed
by the way Campbell had defeated the prominent president of
the NDP. Besides being personally committed to elevating women
to high office, Mulroney had another reason to promote
Campbell's career: he considered the other Tory MPs from British
Columbia dismal cabinet material. "I would be surprised if I
wasn't in consideration but it's a matter for the prime minister to
decide," Campbell said in early December.

Although concern for regional representation obligated
Mulroney to include both Tom Siddon and Frank Oberle in his
cabinet, neither of these B.C. MPs threatened to upstage
Campbell. In 1985, Siddon had enraged Mulroney when he strut-
ted into the Commons wearing a flowing graduation gown while
Finance Minister Michael Wilson was giving an important
speech that retreated from the plan to de-index old age pensions.
A horrified Mulroney spotted Siddon sitting proudly in his robes
directly behind Wilson. "Get that fucking thing off," he shouted,
and Siddon skittered to the government lobby. While Oberle had
never done anything so ridiculous, he was still not respected by
the prime minister.

Campbell and Eddy settled into Carney's $1,200-a-month apartment in Ottawa, where Eddy soon found a job as a lawyer for the Immigration and Refugee Board. Kim brought her favorite books, her Inuit carvings and a Sam Black print of Vancouver harbor. The couple also purchased a set of dishes for entertaining senior politicians and bureaucrats.

The first sign that Campbell was destined for a cabinet post came on December 12, when Mulroney asked her and rookie Quebec MP Gilles Loiselle to respond to the Speech from the Throne. Loiselle was a former Parti Québécois bureaucrat who had orchestrated his province's campaign against Pierre Trudeau's 1982 constitution while serving in London. He and Campbell were made from the same mold: both considered themselves intellectuals and possessed great ambition.

Except for reviewing the benefits of free trade and praising John Fraser, Campbell's speech on December 12, 1988, was very similar to her maiden address before the B.C. legislature in which she discussed the diversity of her riding and talked about how proud she felt to be part of the institution. Mulroney stayed in his seat throughout both Campbell's and Loiselle's speeches to demonstrate that he believed they were bound for more important positions than the ones they occupied on the back benches. He was startled when Campbell burst into French midway through her speech. "She speaks French!" he exclaimed.

One evening a month later, Campbell received the phone call she was expecting. She was in her apartment when one of Mulroney's aides instructed her to report to 24 Sussex Drive at 7:45. Although it seemed odd to her that Mulroney would want to see her so early in the morning, Campbell brushed off the thought. Her father and stepmother were in town and she cheerfully suggested that they all step out for a late dinner. On her return, she was surprised to receive a frantic message from Stanley Hartt, Mulroney's chief of staff. "Where are you?" Hartt demanded. "The prime minister was expecting you at 7:45. Now he's gone back to Harrington Lake, so he'll have to call you from up there. But he was very worried about you and he called the commissioner of the RCMP to see if they could find you." As Hartt spoke, Campbell later told *Vancouver Magazine*, she "was thinking 'Oh God, what a turkey'—[Mulroney] must be rethinking whether he should be planning anything with me at all. In the end he did call me and he was unbelievably sweet."

On January 30, 1989, Mulroney shuffled his cabinet and brought in six new cabinet ministers. Campbell was made minister of state for Indian and Northern Affairs under Quebecker Pierre Cadieux. Siddon became minister of Fisheries and Oceans, Oberle was given Forestry, and Mary Collins was appointed the associate minister of Defence. Siddon became the B.C. minister put in charge of doling out patronage and was named to the powerful 19-member inner cabinet. However, despite these appointments, no one from B.C. sat on the key cabinet committees of Expenditure Review or Operations. This was an inner clique of superministers—Don Mazankowski, Joe Clark, Michael Wilson, Robert de Cotret, Barbara McDougall and Harvie Andre—who controlled the government with their spending clout and input into every policy decision.

Of the 15 cabinet committees, Campbell was seated on three: Human Resources, Income Support and Health, and the Special Committee of Council. Chaired by Deputy Prime Minister Mazankowski, the Special Committee gave her immediate exposure to the detailed work of running government. The council was the clearing-house for every government appointment, every change of regulation and all routine orders dealing with foreign trade.

Although Campbell did not yet have high cabinet rank, she received the same pay, perks and privileges as the crown princes and princesses of government. Her relatively few responsibilities entitled her to a driver and a limousine, a staff of 12 and an array of offices. Campbell's salary and tax-free allowances amounted to more than $130,000 annually, including a $2,000 car subsidy, a leftover from bygone decades when ministers were not provided with chauffeur-driven limousines.

Campbell's appointment to Indian and Northern Affairs upset B.C.'s native leaders, who did not approve of the type of work her husband had done in the provincial ministry of the attorney general. In almost all major cases involving native issues, Eddy had led the legal team trying to prevent the courts from recognizing the existence of aboriginal land claims. Explaining that her husband was only doing his job, Campbell dismissed the natives' concerns. "A lawyer represents his client's position," she said. "It would be a mistake to think otherwise." Although their fears about Eddy's previous work soon dissipated, aboriginal leaders remained suspicious of Campbell's willingness to defend the interests of native people, particularly in the light of a new Conservative policy.

On March 20, 1989, Pierre Cadieux announced that he was putting a cap of $130 million on the Post Secondary Student Assistance Program, which had permitted native students to receive funding for up to eight years of higher education. The new policy would shorten the length of time students could get financial aid, would cut off assistance if they failed courses and would change the amounts allocated to cover their tuition and expenses.

Figures showed that since its inception in the mid-1970s, the program had been very effective in encouraging young natives to raise themselves out of poverty by becoming better educated. In the late 1960s only 3.4 percent of natives finished high school and just a handful went on to university; in 1978, 3,500 native students were enrolled at the post-secondary level. When Cadieux stepped in to restrict the program, the number of students receiving funds had climbed to 15,000. Of the approximately 1,000 natives who received degrees each year, nine out of ten found jobs—a significant statistic given an unemployment rate among natives that reached as high as 90 percent.

Federal officials claimed that the new limits were necessary because the program was being exploited by students who stayed in school year after year without bothering to graduate. Outraged natives, resenting the implication that their sons and daughters were freeloaders, argued that the program was a marvellous success despite a few cases of misuse. They insisted that educational funding was a right granted by treaties signed more than a century ago and claimed that the proposed restrictions would deny about 2,000 aboriginal students admission to college or university in the fall of 1989.

Campbell entered the controversy on the side of Cadieux. She stated that the program could no longer be driven by demand because Ottawa could not afford to support all students who wanted a higher education. In the Commons in April, she defended the minister by arguing that post-secondary educational funding was not a treaty right and that natives should be content that the government deigned to give them any money at all. "The budget cannot continue to expand at the rate of the last decade," she said. "There are no other Canadians who have this assistance from the federal government for post-secondary education. . . . The fact that our philosophic underpinning is not that of the treaty nations, that we do not see it as a treaty obligation, does not mean that we do not see it as a vitally important policy and important part of our desire to see native people assume their rightful role in Canadian society."

It was unclear that any money would be saved overall by capping the program. Critics pointed out that while the Conservative government seemed to be willing to pay $50,000 a year to keep a native in jail, it was balking at allotting $9,000 annually to provide a native student with the education she or he needed to become self-sufficient. Georges Erasmus, of the Assembly of First Nations, saw no reason for the cutbacks. "It makes no sense," he said. "If 90 percent of our people were not lined up for welfare, perhaps you'd talk about controlling the amount of money."

Other aboriginal leaders accused the government of cutting the program just when larger numbers of students were beginning to profit from it. They argued that the new restrictions would rupture a longstanding federal commitment to provide natives with education in exchange for aboriginal lands. Even though free education had not been included in the treaties signed with native chiefs in the nineteenth century, it had been provided for more than a hundred years to many children at the level of residential schools as well as to the few who survived the system to arrive at university.

A hunger strike by 14 native students and a spate of negative publicity eventually forced the government to revise its plans. Cadieux agreed to provide higher allowances and to underwrite native education through the doctoral level; but Campbell's strong defence of the initiative convinced many natives that she was not sympathetic to the needs of Canada's first nations, an opinion reinforced by the speech she delivered in the Commons on April 24, 1989. Although Campbell acknowledged that natives generally face living conditions that are worse than those of other Canadians, she insisted that this was no cause for regret. "Why must there always be this litany of negativism?" she wondered. "Rather, we should take heart in the stunning progress which has occurred over the past generation, and especially in the past ten years. We need historical perspective in order to understand and deal with the remaining problems."

To native Canadians, Campbell's optimism seemed ludicrous. The government had taken a few actions to improve their lot— by granting them the right to vote in 1961, by closing church-run residential schools, by allowing bands greater autonomy and by holding four inconclusive constitutional conferences on self-government—yet these measures did not add up to "stunning progress." A Statistics Canada study revealed that aboriginals were three times more likely to die before age 35 than were other Canadians. Campbell went on to say that although most natives had housing that was seriously inadequate in the 1960s, by 1989, two-thirds of native homes had been equipped with sewers and sep-tic tanks. "Indian living conditions have improved significantly in the last quarter century," she claimed. Many saw her remarks as an attempt to absolve Ottawa of its responsibility toward aboriginal communities.

The Canadian Human Rights Commission was certainly con-cerned about the natives' quality of life. In a report issued the same year that Campbell claimed aboriginals were doing very well, Max Yalden, the head of the commission, wrote that the "situa-tion faced by Canada's native peoples is in many ways a national tragedy." Although some of the social indicators, such as the num-ber of native homes with flush toilets, might have improved, the conditions of aboriginal life were a long way from matching the expectations of Canadian society as a whole. For example, Yalden noted that 10 percent of male and 13 percent of female natives languish in jails even though aboriginals make up only 2 percent of the population. A native youngster had a better chance of be-ing sent to prison than of completing university. "The over-riding problem in all this is our notorious difficulty in coming to grips with native issues in a comprehensive way," he explained, stress-ing that "the important point from the human rights perspective, is to recognize clearly that the time has come to raise this issue to the very highest level of the national agenda."

To her credit, Campbell listened to her advisers and began to approach the settlement of land claims in a more flexible way than she had when she served in the B.C. legislature. Previously, she had followed Bill Bennett and later Bill Vander Zalm in in-sisting that the province negotiate only if Ottawa would agree to pay the cost of any settlement. The government of B.C. had long

Kim Campbell was born in Port Alberni, B.C. Named Avril Phaedra Douglas at birth, she changed her name to Kim at age 12. (George Campbell)

"My sister and I were great tomboys," recalls Campbell. She spent her early childhood in the municipality of Burnaby and later in the Kerrisdale area of Vancouver.
(George Campbell)

Avril and her father, Paul. He changed his name from George at the insistence of his first wife, Lissa. After their break-up, he changed his name back to George.
(George Campbell)

Campbell's classmates and teachers remember her as destined for success. In 1964, at the age of 17, she was the valedictorian of her graduating class at Prince of Wales High School in Vancouver.
(George Campbell)

Campbell was known for her acting and musical abilities. This photo was taken in 1970. At the time, she and her future husband, Tuzie Divinsky, entertained his colleagues with renditions of Gilbert and Sullivan operettas.
(The Vancouver Sun)

Campbell's first foray into politics resulted in her election as a trustee for the Vancouver School Board. This photo was taken at a 1982 meeting; in 1983 she became chairman of the board. (Courtesy of the Vancouver School Board)

In 1986 Campbell made a disastrous bid for the leadership of B.C.'s Social Credit party. Lack of funds didn't stop her from campaigning creatively and giving the contest her best shot. Although she came in dead last, Campbell went on to win the Vancouver/Point Grey riding for the Socreds and a seat in B.C.'s legislature. (The Province)

Her 1988 decision to switch to federal politics paid off in short order. In early 1990, Prime Minister Mulroney elevated Campbell to the position of Justice minister. Here she is shown engaged in a debate on abortion in the House of Commons. (Canapress)

As Defence minister, Campbell was called upon to quell many fires. Despite all the controversy, some say she handled the portfolio with more skill than her predecessor, Marcel Masse. (John Hryniuk)

Campbell returned to her native Vancouver to announce her candidacy for the Tory leadership. During her speech, she attempted to distance herself from Brian Mulroney. (Jeff Vinnick/Reuters)

"All for one and one for all." Conservative leadership candidates Patrick Boyer, Kim Campbell, Garth Turner, Jean Charest and Jim Edwards pose before launching into the first Conservative party leadership debate in April 1993. (Canapress)

On June 13, 1993, Kim Campbell made history, becoming Canada's first woman prime minister designate. "The biggest challenge before us is to win the trust and confidence of Canadians," she told Tory supporters after her 53 percent victory at the leadership convention. (The Toronto Star/R. Bull)

held the view that aboriginal title had been extinguished when the province joined Confederation in 1871. When she was appointed to Indian and Northern Affairs in Ottawa, Campbell adopted a more pragmatic approach. Although she did not propose that B.C. go as far as splitting expenses with Ottawa 50/50, she maintained that Victoria had to pay part of the costs.

According to one senior official in Indian and Northern Affairs, Campbell played a significant part in efforts to resolve the demands of B.C. natives once she was convinced that the province had to join the negotiations. "We were trying to make the government of British Columbia see that in their own best economic interests, they had to deal with this question," he says. "Kim was pretty much the key player, not only in developing the strategy but in getting to the table in the first place." He explains that Campbell and senior adviser Richard Van Loon pushed B.C. to face the issue by arguing that native roadblocks would continue to disrupt logging operations and that violence would erupt if negotiations did not begin. Mounting legal costs from a string of native victories in court reinforced Ottawa's case that it would be wise for B.C. to work out a deal. However, he says, although Campbell had a major role in designing plans for the talks, since she and Vander Zalm were not "bosom buddies," negotiations were left to Cadieux.

In contrast to the view that Campbell worked hard to settle land claims, Ron George, president of the Native Council of Canada, does not believe that she did much to address the longstanding grievances of aboriginal people. He says that unlike Constitutional Affairs Minister Joe Clark, Campbell did not convince native people that she believed in the justice of their cause. When she was minister, George headed B.C.'s United Native Nations, an organization that represents 20,000 off-reserve natives. "She did absolutely nothing for us while she was our interlocutor. Zippo. Nothing," says George. "When she was in B.C. she was basically pointing the finger at Ottawa to pick up the tab for both land claims and off-reserve Métis peoples. When she got into Ottawa she accepted the status quo, looking toward the province to be involved in picking up the tab. It depended on which hat she was wearing."

Chief Joe Mathias of the Squamish Nation says that B.C. natives do not believe that Campbell played a significant role in bringing the province into the process. A key player in the trilateral talks, Mathias says there was little progress on the issue "until the new NDP government got elected and they reversed B.C.'s position." Miles Richardson, president of the Council of the Haida Nation, agrees with Mathias and adds that in general, he found Campbell to be somewhat inflexible about matters that concerned aboriginal people. "I think Kim Campbell is very certain of her view of the world and is very slow to accept that there are other at least equally relevant views of the world," he says.

Although Campbell kept a relatively low profile in the native portfolio during her tenure in Indian and Northern Affairs, she took to the hustings with great enthusiasm to promote the Meech Lake Accord, even though she had neglected to vote for it in B.C. This support for Meech Lake did not win her many friends among natives who had been excluded from the constitutional package.

For the most part, she used her time as a junior cabinet minister to learn the ropes from senior bureaucrats who found her bright, shrewd, tough and approachable. She had the good sense to ask Harry Swain, then deputy minister of Indian and Northern Affairs and a fellow British Columbian, to tutor her about the inner workings of the government. Every Monday morning at nine o'clock, Campbell would meet Swain for an hour of what one official describes as "fairly rigorous" discussions about the functioning of the cabinet system and the nuances of the bureaucracy. "She is a very good student and a very quick learner with a very good mind," says Fred Drummie, the recently retired associate deputy minister, who also acted as tutor. "She soaks up information like a sponge."

Drummie admits that Campbell was not a major initiator of policy at Indian and Northern Affairs, but notes that as a green-horn, she had to get used to Ottawa before she could contribute much to developing new approaches. "She was getting her act together as a minister, period," he remembers. "She was taking French. She was organizing an office in Ottawa and an office in B.C. We didn't realize it at the time, but her marriage was clearly heading for the rocks. We didn't know that, but obviously that must have taken a fair amount of her attention."

In addition to becoming known as a fast learner, Campbell also acquired a reputation for having flexible principles. Her approach to the abortion legislation that was tabled by Justice Minister Doug Lewis in 1989 exemplified what many considered her politics of opportunism. Bill C-43 would make abortion a crime punishable by up to two years in jail unless a doctor determined that a woman would jeopardize her physical or mental health by continuing the pregnancy. The new legislation would greatly restrict access to therapeutic abortion and, in certain cases, make criminals of both the women who obtained abortions and the doctors who performed them.

On the evening of November 21, Campbell rose in the Commons to endorse the legislation that would restore abortion to the Criminal Code. "I am well known as an advocate of those who are pro-choice," she stated. "But I can say quite sincerely and with quite a clear heart that I believe that this bill is actually better than no law." Campbell knew that her stand would cause a stir. "This is a position which will come as a surprise to many people who share my position on the fundamental issue of abortion," she said.

Campbell explained that personally she could live with the status quo in which there was no law restricting abortion. As a parliamentarian, however, she said that she felt an obligation to support a law that represented the consensus of the House of Commons. Campbell told MPs that Bill C-43 would strike a balance between the rights of a woman and those of the unborn child. She wanted doctors involved in the process in order to prevent the tragedy of having a woman go through an abortion that "she later regrets."

Warning that the provinces could restrict access to abortion in the absence of a federal law, Campbell argued that Bill C-43 would establish a "national standard of access to safe, legal, funded abortions" that could be performed in clinics as well as in accredited hospitals. She reasoned that the new law did not place undue restrictions on abortion because it specified that women needed to get approval from only one doctor. Previously, in some areas of the country, women wanting to terminate a pregnancy had to seek permission from a hospital committee.

New Democrat Dawn Black was in the House when Campbell gave her support to the legislation. She contrasts Campbell's calm demeanor with that of Employment Minister Barbara McDougall, who was also obliged to put aside her pro-choice views to back the government. "It was quite a dramatic moment," recalls Black. "Yet when Kim Campbell altered her position, it was very dry. There didn't appear to be any of the personal anguish that I felt with Barbara." Black assumed that Campbell had sold out her personal principles on abortion to guarantee herself a more important cabinet post.

A furious Mary Clancy left the chamber to sit in the opposition lobby when Campbell endorsed the bill. Like Black, she sees Campbell's stand as motivated by ambition. "This is a game in which women have very little power and there are two ways you can address it," she explains. "You can address it by going along with the agenda of those in power who can help you or you can address it by taking your own agenda and fighting every step of the way. Most of the women I know do the second."

Pro-choicers across Canada were enraged at Campbell's support of the bill. Hilda Thomas of the B.C. Coalition of Abortion Clinics called her about-face "indefensible." Other leaders of the women's movement, feeling that Campbell had sold them out, swore that they would neither forget nor forgive her betrayal of feminist principles.

A few months later, Campbell may well have been rewarded for her staunch defence of the government's abortion bill. On February 23, 1990, Mulroney elevated her to the position of minister of Justice, making her the first woman in Canada to serve in this capacity. In her new job as the country's top lawmaker, she would show unusual skill at crafting legislation that would shape her image as a progressive.

6

JUSTICE FOR ALL?

Rape is not sex. Rape is violence where sex is the means to inflict humiliation or dominance or whatever the source of anger or hostility the perpetrator feels toward his victims.

— *Kim Campbell, August 28, 1991*

The huge wrought-iron gates swung open as a midnight blue Crown Victoria rolled up the driveway flanked by mounds of dirty snow. A uniformed Mountie, armed with his machine gun, nodded approval to the chauffeur from a snug perch in the heated, bulletproof gatehouse. It was mid-February, the time when Ottawa ties with Ulan Batar as the coldest capital on earth. On time for her 5:15 appointment, the junior minister of Indian and Northern Affairs rushed up the stone steps through the biting cold into the cozy ambience of 24 Sussex Drive, where she had been invited to discuss her future before accompanying the prime minister to the Commons for an evening vote.

118

At the age of 42, she was about to become the minister of Justice, a high-profile position traditionally reserved for seasoned veterans of government. But Mulroney had more in store for his young protégée. He informed Campbell that he was planning to admit her to his inner cabinet and put her in charge of patronage for British Columbia in place of the clownish Tom Siddon. She would also acquire a fair number of other responsibilities: besides chairing the Ad Hoc Committee on Justice and Legal Affairs, she would sit on the committees of Cultural Affairs and National Identity, Federal–Provincial Relations, and Legislation and House Planning. And, if that was not enough to set her head spinning, saving the best for last, Mulroney announced that she would sit with him on the all-powerful Expenditure Review Committee.

Although the Priorities and Planning Committee, soon to number 21 members, was supposed to function as the inner cabinet, it was too large and unwieldy to cope with the demands of government. The real inner cabinet was the Operations Committee, known as Ops, which decided on all major bills, communication strategies, political planning and damage control. Headed by Deputy Prime Minister Don Mazankowski, this authoritative group was composed of nine senior cabinet ministers: Harvie Andre, Benoît Bouchard, Joe Clark, John Crosbie, Gilles Loiselle, Barbara McDougall, Senator Lowell Murray and Michael Wilson.

Until it was disbanded in January 1993, the second key body was the 10-member Expenditure Review Committee, headed by Mulroney. No minister could get a dollar for new programs without the approval of this influential clique that included all the members of Ops, minus Bouchard, Clark and McDougall. By making her one of these watchdogs, Mulroney was putting Campbell in the inner circle of power, on the omnipotent team that ran the government.

Although Mulroney says that he and Campbell were in his study when he informed her of his plans, she told the Montreal *Gazette* in March 1990 that he broke the news while they were in his limousine speeding along Sussex Drive to Parliament Hill for a vote. "He later told some friends that my eyes got really, really big, and he wasn't sure if it was from surprise or whether I thought he was going to kill me whizzing at top speed through Ottawa," she said. "I wasn't too terribly sure myself."

On February 23, Campbell replaced Doug Lewis as Justice minister. "I'm absolutely thrilled. . . . I can't begin to tell you how excited I am," she said. Mulroney understood that women had much to offer, she told reporters, and that the country had evolved beyond tokenism. "The importance of having strong representation of women in government is because women experience the world differently from men," she explained.

Since Bill C-43 was still before the House of Commons, spokespersons from both sides of the abortion debate had much to say about the promotion. Although feminists applauded the appointment of a female minister of Justice, they were outraged that Campbell had sacrificed her pro-choice principles on the altar of ambition. On the other hand, pro-life groups interpreted her ascent as a feminist takeover of the justice system. "What we had in Doug Lewis was an apologist for the feminists," said Margaret Purcell, vice-president of Campaign Life. "What we have in Kim Campbell is one of the radical feminists themselves."

A master of political tactics, Mulroney demonstrated his shrewdness with Campbell's timely appointment. With the exception of capital punishment, he knew the matter of abortion would prove to be the most divisive issue his government would face. Campbell was the perfect choice to steer C-43 through Parliament: as an avowed pro-choicer, she could persuade Canadians to compromise on an issue that defied consensus. And her previous support for the bill in the House indicated that she was onside. He hoped she would work her magic quickly so that the government could focus on instituting a 7 percent goods and services tax, a measure that could be expected to generate enormous protest.

Days after moving to the frontlines of cabinet, Campbell began an aggressive campaign to make the C-43 bill into law. Just as Mulroney was to do when he pitched Meech Lake to Canadians, Campbell warned of the dangers of not passing C-43. "It is unlikely that it would be possible to gain consensus for another bill," she said. Without a federal law, she argued, the provinces could limit access to abortion with draconian measures. "If the provinces choose to exercise their jurisdiction in a way that would be restrictive to access to abortion, then it's out of the federal government's hands," she stated ominously.

Opponents of C-43 claimed that Canadians were being deceived. Stating that Campbell was trying to "paint Bill C-43 in pro-choice hues," Professor Bruce Ryder of Osgoode Hall Law School pointed out that recriminalizing abortion would limit women's access while doing nothing to prevent the provinces from imposing further restrictions. If Ottawa was serious about guaranteeing access, he said, it could have used its power under the Canada Health Act to withhold funds from any province that interfered with abortion.

Former Supreme Court justice Bertha Wilson, who sat on the Court when it struck down the old abortion law, was appalled by what Campbell said to support the bill. She found the Justice minister's suggestion that women needed advice from doctors to make the right choice about terminating pregnancy to be as insulting to Canadians' intelligence as the claim that recriminalizing abortion would make it safer. "I've got complete confidence that women can make those decisions," said Wilson. "I mean, if they are fit to procreate then they surely must be fit to decide what to do in a situation like that. . . . If you put restrictions back in the Criminal Code you are going to restore the backroom abortions."

Doctors were worried that pro-life crusaders would drag them into court since C-43 had such vague guidelines about what constituted a lawful abortion. Although the act allowed for abortion when a doctor was of the opinion that continuing the pregnancy would threaten a woman's physical, mental or psychological health, no definition of the word "health" was provided and no criteria were established for determining whether the opinion had been based on "accepted standards of the medical profession." The Canadian Medical Association and the Society of Obstetricians and Gynecologists of Canada did not accept Campbell's assurance that the legislation would not be used to harass doctors: the association argued that pro-lifers could lay criminal charges against those who performed abortions and warned that if C-43 became law, as many as 268 physicians, a significant number, would refuse to do abortions.

Campbell's efforts to sell the bill as a compromise also displeased the pro-life faction who saw the proposed legislation as abortion on demand. Anti-choice groups asserted that the bill did nothing to protect the rights of the fetus. They said C-43 would allow anyone to get an abortion since all that was required was a doctor's statement that carrying the fetus to term could jeopardize a woman's health. In their view, the proposed law put a criminal aura around abortion, but it didn't go far enough. It would be possible to bring doctors to court without setting any guidelines for prosecution.

Pro-life Conservative and Liberal MPs were unable to pressure Campbell to amend the bill to enshrine rights for the unborn; but Tory backbenchers forced Mulroney to allow a free vote according to conscience. Unsure of how the vote would go, Mulroney commanded the 37 members of his cabinet to back the legislation. Staunch pro-life ministers such as Benoît Bouchard and Jake Epp betrayed their principles and heeded the boss's order so that they could maintain their cabinet rank—an act that many thought paralleled Campbell's support of the bill.

A hush fell over the Commons on May 29 when Campbell rose to vote in favor of C-43. Moments later pandemonium broke

out: "No new law. You're making us criminals!" screamed pro-
choice advocates in the visitors' gallery as they hurled skirts im-
printed with the words "Choice Now" onto the floor of the
chamber. Outside the building, pro-lifers sang hymns. In the final
tally, the bill squeaked through by a vote of 140 to 131. Campbell
had won a victory and had every reason to believe C-43 would
become the law of the land.

Now the field of battle moved to the Senate, which opted to hear
the opinions of Canadian citizens. The committee that was assigned
this mission studied 300 letters or briefs and interviewed 38 witnesses.
Only four backed the bill: representatives from the Law Reform
Commission; delegates from the religious sect known as the Plymouth
Brethren; and Campbell and Health Minister Perrin Beatty.

While the committee was holding hearings, a Nova Scotia
court handed down a decision that heartened pro-choice advocates by demolishing a central argument Campbell had used to
support the bill. Even though there was no federal abortion law,
the court struck down a provincial statute that restricted abortions, on the grounds that it intruded on federal jurisdiction.
Campbell's claim that a federal law was needed to prevent the
provinces from limiting access to abortion was proven false.

On February 1, 1991, the usually empty Upper Chamber was
packed to the rafters as the abortion bill that pleased almost no one
went down to defeat by a tie vote of 43 to 43. Despite last-minute
appeals by Campbell and Conservative Senate Leader Lowell
Murray, eight Tory senators—including Pat Carney, who had flown
in from Vancouver—joined the Liberals to defeat the bill.
Spectators in the Senate celebrated the demise of C-43 with laughter and whoops of joy. "Abortion is legal and it will be legal for a
generation," said an exultant Judy Rebick, president of the National
Action Committee on the Status of Women. Anti-abortion cam-
paigner Rev. Kenneth Campbell described the defeat as both a
tragedy and a triumph: "We opposed the bill because it sought to

institutionalize the killing of innocent pre-born. . . . It is better to have no bill at all."

Although there were some who thought that the unelected Senate should not have thwarted the will of the House of Commons, most commentators felt that the Senate had acted wisely in crushing an unnecessary bill that clashed with the Supreme Court's 1988 ruling. If C-43 had become law, it would have contravened Chief Justice Brian Dickson's judgment that "forcing a woman, by threat of criminal sanctions, to carry a fetus to term unless she meets certain criteria unrelated to her own priorities and aspirations" was an interference with a woman's body.

Campbell was a good sport about the defeat: "Parliament has spoken. Democracy has worked," she said. However, despite this dignified acceptance of the vote, she had suffered a major setback. Since Mulroney had been unable to persuade a sufficient number of Tory senators to support the bill, he could not fault her for her efforts. But by putting her heart and soul into the attempt to recriminalize abortion, Campbell had lost the respect of an increasingly influential feminist constituency.

In the midst of the controversy about abortion, Campbell was called upon to make good on Mulroney's longstanding promise to tighten up Canada's gun control laws. Two months before she was named minister of Justice, Marc Lepine had set off on a deadly mission. Armed with a high-powered semi-automatic rifle, he massacred 14 female engineering students at Montreal's Ecole Polytechnique before killing himself. In the suicide note, discovered later at his apartment, Lepine blamed feminists for all the failures in his life. Canadians were horrified at the bloodbath.

The massacre was a catalyst for more than half a million people who signed petitions demanding more restrictions on firearms. Yet, even in the aftermath of the grisly shootings, Doug Lewis, Campbell's predecessor, had promised only modest changes to the existing law: he would ban imports of military assault rifles, such as the Israeli-made Uzi and the Soviet-designed AK-47, but would not impose more stringent controls on semi-automatic weapons and handguns.

In mid-April, during a visit to the Ecole Polytechnique, Campbell defended the tepid legislation: "It's a little simplistic to say we should ban semi-automatic weapons," she told the dejected students. "As nobody knows better than engineering students, there's always a way to tinker with a weapon to make it more advanced." Proponents of gun control showed that her logic was seriously flawed. Since it is easy to convert a semi-automatic weapon to a fully automatic one, but next to impossible to turn a bolt-action rifle into a semi-automatic, outlawing semi-automatics would make a great deal of sense.

Campbell was widely criticized for repeating the refrain of the pro-gun lobby that problems were caused by people and not by weapons. Editorials argued that certain types of firearms encouraged acts of extreme violence. "Semi-automatics' prime function," said the Montreal *Gazette*, "is slaughter. For what else would people need a weapon that, if the firer changes magazines rapidly, can fire up to 80 bullets per minute?"

Just before Parliament recessed for the summer, Campbell introduced legislation that attempted to placate those who wanted the new controls to be stronger. Bill C-90 would prohibit large magazines—like the one Lepine used on his semi-automatic Sturm Ruger rifle—by permitting only five-round clips for rifles and ten-shot magazines for handguns. Specific combat weapons and semi-automatic rifles that could easily be made fully automatic would be banned, and anyone who wanted a firearm licence would be required to pass a safety course.

Bill C-90 riled hunters, trappers, gun collectors and Conservative members of Parliament from rural Canada. A delegation of 30 MPs, led by Felix Holtmann from Manitoba, mounted a ferocious campaign to kill the legislation. By fall, when the House was back in session, Campbell had lost control of the process despite promises from Liberals and New Democrats to give C-90 quick approval. Vigorous lobbying by gun enthusiasts had persuaded rural Tory backbenchers to dig in their heels. In November, unable to win converts in caucus, Campbell shelved the controversial bill by referring it to a special Commons committee. "I have received a great many representations from firearm owners," she explained. Two weeks later a hypocritical government paid tribute to the 14 women who had died in Lepine's rampage.

Faced with a recalcitrant caucus, Campbell tried hard to find a compromise. She toyed with the awkward solution of enacting two separate gun laws: urban residents could be compelled to store guns in a secure central depot while less restrictive measures could apply to those who lived in rural areas. Every week she held meetings with the most vocal opponents of gun control, such as Albert Cooper, Bill Domm, Felix Holtmann, John MacDougall, John Reimer and Dave Worthy. "She said, 'Look, we won't move with the thing until I meet with you,'" recalls Bob Horner, the MP from Mississauga West who chairs the Commons Justice Committee. Even though he favored swift passage of tougher restrictions on firearms, Horner believes that Campbell had little choice but to work with the dissident MPs who had a great number of gun enthusiasts in their ridings. "So she'd hold a meeting and they'd go away and she'd bring it to caucus again," he remembers. "There would be dissatisfaction and so she'd hold another meeting, and she did that until she got people onside."

In May 1991, Campbell unveiled her second attempt at strengthening Canada's gun laws. Although current owners of Uzis or AK-47s would be allowed to keep their weapons, Bill C-17 would ban or restrict all other military-style assault rifles; fully automatic weapons would be outlawed after a fixed date; and a committee of experts would decide about the size of clips. The bill also established regulations about the purchase of firearms: a 28-day waiting period would be imposed between the time a person applied to buy a gun and the issuing of a permit; all gun owners would have to meet regulations concerning the safe storage of weapons; and anyone convicted of a serious crime would be unable to own a gun for ten years. The legislation did not ban semi-automatic rifles like the type used by Lepine. "I can't guarantee it would have stopped him," Campbell admitted. "But it would have put up some barriers."

Gun-loving MPs disliked certain aspects of the new bill, but most agreed to support the minister's latest effort. Campbell touted the legislation as tougher than C-90. "Today is a wonderful day for me because I feel somewhat vindicated," she told reporters. Gun control lobbyists strongly disagreed. "To present this as a tough gun control bill is patently ridiculous," complained Wendy Cukier, president of the Coalition for Gun Control. Suzanne Laplante-Edwards, whose daughter Anne-Marie was killed by Lepine, said she felt "betrayed by our government." However, Laplante-Edwards and other gun control advocates conceded that they had little choice but to support C-17. "We will support this bill because . . . we don't want blood on our hands," said Heidi Rathjen, head of the Polytechnique Gun Control Committee.

In late June, Campbell faced another disappointment. The bill could not be passed before the summer recess. She asked a Tory-dominated Commons committee to finish its hearings so that C-17 could be adopted when Parliament resumed in mid-September, but committee chairman Blaine Thacker said more hearings would be needed. Campbell was angry: "I seem to be the only one here with a sense of urgency in getting it passed," she said. She would have to wait until the second anniversary of the Montreal massacre before Bill C-17 cleared the Senate and was enacted into law.

In the summer of 1992, about six months after the bill had passed, Campbell supplied details about how the law would work in practice. The most deadly guns, such as the Universal Enforcer, Bushmaster Pistol and the Striker 12 Streetsweeper, would be banned;

200 types of semi-assault weapons, such as the AK-47, would be restricted by the requirement that owners get a special certificate to own, transport and use them. Buyers of guns would have to pay a $50 fee for a Firearms Acquisition Certificate and applicants would need references from two guarantors. While magazines for handguns would be limited to ten shots and only five-round clips would be permitted in semi-automatic rifles, no restrictions would be placed on the magazines of the bolt-action Lee Enfield and the semi-automatic .22.

Although Lepine's Sturm Ruger could still be purchased over the counter under the conditions specified in the new legislation, gun control advocates and police hailed the regulations as a significant advance. "It's quite a victory, no question about that," Laplante-Edwards said. Although he was puzzled about why the AK-47 was not banned outright, Ottawa Police Chief Tom Flanagan called the regulations a "giant step forward."

The gun lobby disagreed with these positive responses. Ernie Sopsich, executive director of the Shooting Federation of Canada, described the regulations as "just a politically correct response that doesn't focus on the criminal misuse of firearms."

Even though she irked many gun enthusiasts, Campbell received much praise for pushing the legislation through Parliament. Those who favored restrictions pointed out that her regulations went beyond the bill by adding the requirement that weapons be kept unloaded and separate from ammunition. She also got credit for resisting pressure from gun lobbyists and MPs in her own party to water down the proposals any further. Although 847,000 Canadians have gun permits and each year there are still 1,300 deaths caused by firearms—200 homicides and 1,100 suicides—C-17 is considered a big advance in public safety. No greater compliment could have been paid to Campbell's efforts than that given by Laplante-Edwards: "Ms. Campbell is very tenacious. . . . She has shown determination and I bow my head to her."

The fact that Campbell had overcome great odds to enact a gun law was of no consequence to feminists such as Shelagh Day of the National Action Committee on the Status of Women. "It is not enough to say Kim Campbell wears a skirt—she has to demonstrate leadership on issues that matter to women," Day said. She spoke for many feminists who strongly disapproved of the minister of Justice for supporting the abortion law and for pushing through legislation they believed was a sell-out to the gun lobby.

In June 1991, Campbell had begun efforts to win over Canadian feminists by organizing a $350,000 symposium in Vancouver called Women, Law and the Administration of Justice. More than 225 members of the justice system, including judges, criminal lawyers, law professors, social workers, poverty activists and police officers, were invited to take part in three days of brainstorming. Their objective was to figure out how to remove male bias from the judicial system so that women could be better protected from violence. For years feminists had been saying that the agencies for abused children, the homes for battered women and the rape crisis centres that had been established over the past decade were stop-gap measures; they wanted more effective ways of dealing with men who assault women and children.

At the conference, judges and lawyers had an opportunity to meet the victims of male violence in a setting other than a courtroom. They talked to poor women struggling to feed their families, to workers in rape crisis centres and to nurses who cared for battered women. When asked how sexism in the justice system could be eliminated, participants recommended that women be involved in the drafting of new laws and that judges—most of whom are middle-aged white males—undergo training in gender sensitivity. Feminists thought that Campbell's symposium was a step in the right direction. "The conference she had in Vancouver was good because it showed a willingness to reach out," says University of Calgary law professor Kathleen Mahoney. However, while activists were delighted that Campbell had sought out their views, they wondered if she would act on their recommendations.

Two months later, in late August, Campbell was given the chance to put words into action when the Supreme Court of Canada struck down the 1983 rape shield law on the grounds that it violated the rights of the accused to a fair trial. The majority decision of seven to two was written by Justice Beverley McLachlin, a former law professor who had taught Campbell. In the ruling, the high court objected to the provision that narrowly limited the circumstances under which a woman could be questioned about her previous sexual history. Judges could now use new criteria to decide whether to allow evidence of past sexual history to be heard in court: evidence could not be used to show that a woman is "less worthy of belief as a witness," and the value of hearing the evidence had to be considered greater than its potential for rendering the trial unfair.

In an 86-page dissenting opinion, Justice Claire L'Heureux-Dubé mounted a strong defence of the old law. She claimed that a woman would be less likely to report a rape if she knew that her sexual history would be open for discussion. Since statistics show that a woman is raped in Canada every 17 minutes, she argued that in the case of rape, it was acceptable to "override the right of the accused" to ensure that perpetrators be charged. Moreover, she said that because judges have shown they are not immune from existing "myths and stereotypes" about women and rape, evidence of past sexual history tended to be "highly prejudicial" to the cases of rape victims.

Feminists complained that the Supreme Court was making it even more difficult for victims of sexual assault to get justice. They pointed out that since the Criminal Code does not define consent, if discussion of a victim's past sexual activity was permitted in court, a man charged with rape might be allowed to argue that his knowledge of the woman's past led him to believe she had consented to sexual intercourse. A rapist could defend himself against a charge of sexual assault by saying that he was too drunk to know a woman had not agreed to have sex on a particular occasion, or by claiming that he believed he had been given consent from the woman's husband, boyfriend or pimp.

Campbell's first instinct was to ask Parliament to codify judicial guidelines in rape cases, but she quickly bowed to requests from women's groups to let them draft a new law. In early September, Campbell invited members of the National Action Committee on the Status of Women, the Women's Legal Education and Action Fund and the National Association of Women and the Law to come to Ottawa to give her advice about formulating rape shield legislation.

A second meeting in October, at which Campbell was not present, turned into a heated affair as about 40 groups—feminist organizations, the Canadian Bar Association, the Canadian Nurses Association and the anti-feminist lobby known as REAL Women—clashed with one another. Lawyers for the Department of Justice disagreed with feminists who insisted that a new rape law must reflect the sexual equality provisions of the Charter of Rights in addition to protecting the rights of the accused to a fair trial. "That was a very confrontational meeting," recalls Queen's University law professor Sheila McIntyre. "Women's groups had caucused and agreed that simply codifying the decision meant nothing. The rules were there. The courts were bound by them. We didn't need Parliament to fix them in stone. We unanimously recommended to slow down, start from first principles and work from equality guarantees in the Charter to law reform rather than working around the edges."

Fearing that their opinions would be either ignored or misrepresented, feminist leaders asked Campbell to meet with them. They told her that piecemeal tinkering with judicial guidelines was unacceptable; the new law must define consent and change the rules about an accused's use of the defence of mistake; a preamble to the law had to explicitly mention women's equality rights and clearly state that past sexual history was rarely relevant and inherently prejudicial. "We came ready for an awful brawl in the sense that we would be positioned as the national feminist movement fighting the introduction of a rape law unless there were substantive changes," says McIntyre. But Campbell "had the nerve to agree to this and see the wisdom while her staff did not, and that was a big shift."

In mid-December, Campbell introduced a bill that explicitly instructed the courts not to acquit on the grounds that a man honestly believed a woman had consented. An accused could not use drunkenness as a defence and would be required to show that he took "all reasonable steps . . . to ascertain that the complainant was consenting." The proposed legislation made it clear that evidence of a woman's sexual history "is rarely relevant" in a rape trial. If defence lawyers wanted to refer to a woman's past, they were required to submit their evidence at a private hearing before a judge. The jury would hear the evidence only if the judge decided it was critical to the defence.

In a rare show of unanimity, all three federal parties voted for the new rape law on second reading. They judged it to be a well-thought-out piece of legislation that clarified once and for all that "no means no." (In the past some judges had stated that no could mean maybe.) "Men who respect women have nothing to fear in any shape or form from this law," New Democrat Dawn Black told the Commons. She said it applied to "only men who force themselves on women, who don't care what women feel or think, [or] who think they have some God-given right to have sex with any woman that they choose at any time."

Surprisingly, the Conservative caucus was supportive of Campbell's far-reaching effort in the bill to strike a balance between the rights of the accused and those of the accuser. REAL Women predictably came out against the legislation, accusing Campbell of pushing through an anti-male law that was part of the radical feminist agenda. However, the loudest outcry came from criminal lawyers. The Ontario Criminal Lawyers Association charged that Bill C-49 was trying to change "centuries of accepted behavior" by requiring men, who are sexual initiators, "to obtain a woman's consent at each stage of the relationship." Brian Greenspan, chair of the Canadian Council of Criminal Defence Lawyers, said the bill would require men to keep hand-held breathalyzers by their bedsides.

Other members of the legal establishment joined the chorus against the legislation. Toronto civil rights lawyer Clayton Ruby said the law would require a conviction if there was any expression of a lack of agreement: "What happens if someone honestly, but mistakenly, believes that when the conduct is viewed as a whole, despite the verbal 'no,' he has an agreement?" Alan Borovoy, head of the Canadian Civil Liberties Association, raised concerns about the way the law treated defences of drunkenness and reasonable belief; he warned that the new proposals could apply to teenage petting or to someone aggressively trying to kiss a woman.

Campbell responded to these arguments in a speech to the Commons on June 15. "It does not require that written consent forms be signed before sexual activity or that a third party be present as an observer to ensure that consent was given; it does not prohibit sexual activity between an employer and an employee, nor does it permit a person to wake up in the morning and revoke the consent given to the previous evening's sexual encounter," she explained. As a sop to the lawyers who opposed the bill, Campbell agreed to delete the word "all" from the clause that required a man to take "all reasonable steps" to ensure that consent had been given.

Campbell earned praise from feminist lawyers and experts on judicial matters for involving them in the process that led to the creation of C-49. "I think the most interesting aspect of that was the fact that she decided to bring in all women's groups to hear from them before she started thinking about legislation," said

Bertha Wilson. "For the first time in my life as a legal person," says Kathleen Mahoney, "I felt like I was part of the system, the power structure and having input. I felt like I was treated in a way that was commensurate with the way most men expect to be treated. I must say that is not a feeling that women have very often in dealing with male-dominated organizations with men at the top."

Campbell also won kudos from feminists when she instituted gender sensitivity courses for federal judges, a recommendation that had been made at her first conference about women and the law. The initiative was supported by an all-party Commons committee that cited concerns about lenient sentences in cases of sexual and spousal assault and called for mandatory training for judges. The National Action Committee on the Status of Women also recommended such training as a means of rooting out anti-female bias in the judiciary.

Explaining that she did not want to interfere with the independence of judges, Campbell ruled out a mandatory program. "I am not interested in imposing on the judiciary a series of politically correct responses," Campbell told journalist Stephen Bindman. "I am not interested in judicial education to try to determine the substantive outcome of what judges decide. What I want is to make sure that judges have the tools they need to do justice. One hopes that with the appropriate judicial education, then true justice will be done and every Canadian that goes to court, whether as a complainant or an accused, [will know] that the person on the bench has all the tools needed to understand what's before him or her."

Campbell's efforts to be seen as an advocate for women were frustrated in February 1992, when Finance Minister Don Mazankowski took an axe to virtually every department in his first budget. To save $22 million a year, Mazankowski eliminated 46 agencies, boards and advisory commissions. The Justice department lost the Law Reform Commission, which had provided long-range legal advice for 21 years.

Women's groups were particularly incensed over the decision to scrap the popular Court Challenges Program. Established in 1985 to help women, minorities, the poor and the disabled to secure their rights under the Charter of Rights and Freedoms, the program provided up to $35,000 for each court challenge. With a five-year budget of $13.5 million, Court Challenges had dealt with more than 300 cases involving equality rights. Its cancellation closed the door on groups such as the Women's Legal Education and Action Fund that had promoted this litigation.

Bertha Wilson sent a letter to Campbell to protest the elimination of "this very imaginative and worthwhile program," which had provided women and minority groups with the means to assert their rights. Campbell ignored her appeal. "She made a terrible mistake there and I don't know why she did it," says Wilson. "I wrote to her because it was wrong. As I said to her, there is no point in giving rights to people if you don't give them the wherewithal to have access to enforce them. I'll never understand why she went along with cutting that, because it was peanuts in terms of money."

Campbell's explanations for eliminating the program were unconvincing. Declaring in the Commons that Ottawa was "the only level of government that has been willing to fund these kinds of cases," she implied that Court Challenges might not have been cut if the provinces had also participated. She also said that Canadians were relying too much on the courts to settle political issues: "There wasn't a mechanism for approaching government to see whether we would make these changes ourselves."

When groups affected by the cuts met with Campbell to register their dissent, she treated them with disdain. Shelagh Day says the minister of Justice was "extremely arrogant and rude" in defending the cancellation of the program as a "fiscal" decision. She recalls that Campbell "put down everyone who was there and was so disrespectful of all these concerned people that it was extremely offensive."

Women's groups were told privately that Campbell had not known the program would disappear. Although she sat on the cabinet's Expenditure Review Committee, her officials said Court Challenges had been axed while the minister was out of the room. "I was told by someone who was there that she did not know until the next day when it was done and that she was absolutely furious," says Kathleen Mahoney.

Despite this interesting rumor, it is improbable that Mazankowski would have scrapped Court Challenges without Campbell's approval. One minister who sat on Expenditure Review said that although he could not remember the discussion that led to eliminating the program, he could not imagine that Campbell, who was known to be "very tough and outspoken," would have been kept ignorant of the cut until the day of the budget. Sheila McIntyre, who studies the Ministry of Justice closely, says that "there is no evidence that Campbell fought for Court Challenges."

It is likely that Campbell did not put up a fuss when the decision was made to cancel Court Challenges because she sympathized with those in the Tory caucus who wanted to get rid of it. "Christ, it was costing a lot of money," says Bob Horner. "It's an attempt to get away from the special-interest groups that will challenge anything just to promote their own self-interest."

The most contentious issue that Campbell faced during her term as Justice minister concerned rights for gays and lesbians. Max Yalden, head of the Canadian Human Rights Commission, had urged the Tories to amend human rights laws to protect gays and lesbians instead of letting the courts determine their rights. In a series of far-reaching proposals, which also addressed other minority groups, he suggested prohibiting discrimination based on sexual orientation or political belief; abolishing mandatory retirement provisions; and taking measures to accommodate the special needs of disabled people as well as those belonging to religious and ethnic minorities.

Since 1985 the Tories had promised to amend the Canadian Human Rights Act to include homosexuals, but no action had yet been taken. However, in 1992, the Ontario Court of Appeal forced the government's hand when it ruled that the rights of homosexuals should be included in the human rights act that covered federal employees.

Campbell stated that she had demonstrated "inclusive justice" when she consulted with women's groups before drafting the rape shield law. Yet, despite her professed commitment to the goal of inclusion, when it came time to draft amendments to the Human Rights Act, gay and lesbian groups were largely excluded from the process. Although Campbell did invite 50 representatives of various constituencies to a consultative meeting about the amendments, she gave participants only six days' notice to prepare themselves for the highly complex discussions that involved gay rights as well as matters concerning the disabled, pay equity and the Indian Act. "People at the meeting decided the whole process was hopeless," Kathleen Ruff, former chair of a federal panel on equality rights, told *The Canadian Forum*. "There was no time to prepare for it, no information to go on, no means provided to examine the proposals."

Conservative MPs had no problem with amendments dealing with the disabled and mandatory retirement, but they were reluctant to extend rights to homosexuals. Members of the so-called Family Caucus, a group of MPs who espouse conservative religious values, vigorously resisted Campbell's efforts to add gay rights to the federal legislation. Defence Minister Marcel Masse had already faced the wrath of this group when he announced that the government would let gays into the military. "I wouldn't want to be stuck in a foxhole in Korea with some gay," fumed one right-wing MP. "Maybe I'm going to be in there for 24 hours." Barbara Greene, the MP from Don Valley North, jumped to her feet in caucus to respond to this homophobic rant: "Here's a guy who is known to all the secretaries on the Hill as 'hands.' He's been feeling up all the girls and now he's afraid some gay is going to feel him up in a foxhole."

Campbell trod lightly on the issue of gay rights, carefully explaining to the largely male caucus that it was far better for Parliament to establish the scope of homosexual rights than to leave it to the courts. She explained that the amendments would not affect everyone in society but would apply only to civil servants and those covered by the federal human rights act, such as employees of banks, airlines and broadcast companies. To allay concerns even further, Campbell promised that the legislation would define marriage as a union between male and female partners. Nevertheless, her arguments were not effective. "The extreme right wing of the caucus thought this was the thin edge of the wedge," recalls Bob Horner, who favors gay rights. "They said if you give gays this much they'll take a mile. The first thing you know is that you'll be into homosexual marriage and tax exemptions and all this type of stuff."

On December 10, 1992, when Parliament was marking Human Rights Day, Campbell tabled legislation to end discrimination on the basis of sexual orientation. The bill did not recognize same-sex marriages and thus denied medical benefits, pension rights, spousal retirement contributions and immigration provisions to gay and lesbian couples. Gay activists were furious: "Campbell can marry several times or live with a man for just one year and they would qualify for the very generous benefits she enjoys as an MP while my lifelong partner gets nothing," complained Vancouver gay activist Steven Hammond. Phillip MacAdam, a human rights lawyer, charged the Tories with "trying to entrench some sort of nineteenth-century vision of the family which is long outmoded."

Bill Domm, Tory MP for Peterborough, Ontario, was a leader in the fight against gay rights. An advocate of capital punishment and a pro-lifer, Domm saw homosexuality as degenerate.

He and other MPs had become alarmed at the growing movement to extend greater rights to minority groups through the
Canadian Human Rights Commission. "I don't think that we
should have blacks, Chinese, gays and lesbians all defined in the
human rights code," he said. "It can be handled by the Charter."
Kitchener MP John Reimer said human rights law should protect
only people who incurred prejudice because of characteristics
they could not change, such as skin color and disabilities:
"Homosexuality is changeable. That fact is indisputable.
Thousands of homosexual men and women have abandoned the
homosexual lifestyle and changed."

Campbell did her best to persuade the Family Caucus to support the legislation. Although she tried to be diplomatic, on at
least one occasion she lost her temper in an exchange with
Domm. "She phoned me and said how important it was for her
and she needed it and was going to get it," Domm recalls. "She
said if she didn't get it she'd resign. I said, 'If you get it I might
have to resign' and she slammed the phone down."

Fredericton MP Bud Bird was one of Campbell's allies in the
caucus. He had a lost a son to AIDS and made an emotional but ul-
timately fruitless appeal to his colleagues to support the legislation.

Finally, Mulroney came to Campbell's defence. Many attribute
the prime minister's sensitivity to homosexual rights to the fact
that his younger brother Gary is gay. Bob Horner recalls the logic
Mulroney used to support Campbell's bill: "He said, 'Fine, there
are gays in society. There is no problem with that. Where do gays
come from?' And this is what hit me. He said, 'Well, they come
from heterosexual parents like you and me. Now if your son and
daughter happened to be gay or lesbian and was refused a job
with the federal government, would you get upset? Goddamn
right you would. You'd be mad as hell.'"

Yet even the prime minister was unable to heal the rift in his
caucus. Many MPs, particularly those from rural areas, did not

want to go into an election having to defend gay rights legislation to the voters. They felt that REAL Women and Reform Party candidates were sure to use the issue to accuse the government of having a feminist and homosexual agenda.

Despite all the opposition Campbell faced, there are those who say that she could have pushed the human rights legislation through the House had she split the bill and allowed a free vote on the contentious issue of gay rights. Since members of the Family Caucus wanted to vote for the provisions dealing with the disabled, they would have had no objections to splitting up the legislation. Horner said the bill would easily have passed because the Family Caucus did not have enough votes to kill the amendments concerned with gay rights. "Twenty or so dissidents would stand up and vote against it, but the Liberals and NDP are going to vote for it anyway, so what the hell was the difference? You win. She could have gotten it through had she split the bill." However, Horner adds that a senior official in the Justice department told him that Campbell was overruled in cabinet when she argued that the legislation should be split.

Failure to get human rights legislation passed tarnished Campbell's image as a highly competent minister. In addition, many criticized her for the way she responded to requests for retrials and demands for compensation. The most famous retrial that occurred during Campbell's tenure as Justice minister was that of David Milgaard, who had been imprisoned for the 1969 slaying of Gail Miller, a nurse's aide from Saskatchewan. Some lawyers who studied the case felt that Milgaard would likely have been paroled had he admitted to the murder instead of maintaining his innocence. Winnipeg lawyer David Asper, Liberal MP John Harvard and Tory Felix Holtmann tried to persuade Campbell to grant a retrial to take account of new findings that witnesses had fabricated evidence against Milgaard. Believing the advice of her department that Milgaard was guilty, Campbell was impervious to all appeals.

Joyce Milgaard was determined to free her son on the basis of a pathologist's report that cast doubt on the conviction. In May 1990, she caught up with Campbell, who was delivering a speech in support of Meech Lake at a Winnipeg luncheon. "I'm sorry, but if you want your son to have a fair hearing, don't approach me personally," Campbell said, leaving Joyce in stunned silence. Her attitude contrasted sharply with the way Brian Mulroney treated Mrs. Milgaard when she cornered him a year later in Winnipeg. Mulroney told her that her son's files would be forwarded to the federal Justice department for immediate review.

Eventually, Milgaard won a retrial and was freed. Holtmann says that if it wasn't for Mulroney's intervention, Milgaard would still be in Manitoba's Stony Mountain Penitentiary. "I had written and asked for a review of David's case far in advance of it ever happening, and it took the prime minister to tell Campbell to review it," he recalls.

Campbell also appeared lax in the way she dealt with compensation for the victims of brainwashing experiments carried out by the CIA at Montreal's Allan Memorial Institute of Psychiatry. Between 1957 and 1964, select patients who were admitted to the hospital became the unwitting victims of a "depatterning" program administered by psychiatrist Ewen Cameron with funds provided by the CIA and the Canadian government. Author Anne Collins, who spent three years researching the subject, wrote that victims were subjected to mind-altering drugs and electroshock treatments that left them "incontinent in both bladder and bowel, unable to dress or feed themselves; they knew neither where they were nor who they were and responded to any stimulus with at most an infantile smile."

In 1990, former B.C. Supreme Court justice Thomas Berger took up the case of one of the victims of the brainwashing experiments. He pleaded with Campbell to provide compensation, reminding her that the CIA had paid $100,000 to each of nine Canadians who had

undergone depatterning. Since the Canadian government had continued to fund the experiments after the CIA withdrew, Berger argued that Ottawa had a responsibility to the victims as well. Nine
months later, Campbell wrote to him stating that the government
had no legal or moral responsibility for the abuse at the clinic. "I
have come to the same conclusion as my predecessors who have reviewed this matter; namely, that the allegations of impropriety
against the government are unfounded," she said.

Faced with a court challenge in November 1992, Campbell reluctantly backed down. The government agreed to pay $100,000 to
each of the estimated 80 men and women who had been subjected
to experiments in Cameron's house of horrors. Campbell continued
to deny that the government had any legal responsibility for the
experiments and noted that the money was being paid purely on
"compassionate and humanitarian grounds." In an editorial, *The
Ottawa Citizen* described Campbell's change of heart as "a small
measure of official regret to Canadians who endured untold misery
because they happened to find themselves in the wrong psychiatric
institution, at the wrong time."

In her handling of both the Milgaard case and the brainwashing scandal, Campbell did not appear to display concern for people who had been badly damaged by the justice system. Unless
she was pushed very hard, she heeded the advice of officials in
the Justice department to keep the ministry's files closed.

Critics say that Campbell's reputation as an activist minister is
undeserved. They point out that she proposed laws only in response to actions by the courts. Judicial decisions instigated the
Jury Act, which allowed the accused in a trial to strike from jury
duty as many people as the Crown does, revision of the defence of
insanity, the rape shield law, and legislation about abortion and
gay rights. In other instances, laws such as the Extradition Act
and one specifying more severe sentences for young offenders were
proposed by the Tory caucus. "Most of the initiatives that we've

had from the Justice minister consist of patching up things that the courts have told us to patch up," says NDP justice critic Ian Waddell. Campbell hotly disputes this charge, insisting that she has been the most pro-active Justice minister in recent times. "I think I really have been a trailblazer," she has said. "I have had a lot of occasions when I could have said, 'Look, let's not do anything about that,' but to suggest it is a lack of leadership because you respond to decisions of the courts is to completely misconceive what the role of the Justice department is. Of course we have to respond. That's our job."

Campbell's high opinion of the work she did as minister of Justice is shared by several experts on Canadian law. David Vienneau, justice reporter for *The Toronto Star*, says that unlike some of her predecessors, Campbell deserves a great deal of praise for responding to court decisions. "I've covered the Justice ministers in this country since Jean Chrétien was the minister and I have no hesitation in saying she has been the most productive, with John Crosbie right behind her," he says.

Sheilah Martin, a law professor at the University of Calgary, agrees that Campbell was a "superb" minister of Justice who made valiant efforts to pass progressive legislation in the face of a recalcitrant caucus. And Erica James, president of the Ontario chapter of the Canadian Bar Association, applauds Campbell both for making substantial progress on women's issues and for opening up channels for future discussion. She believes that "Kim Campbell has been . . . one of the best ministers that we've had. . . . She has enjoyed a level of support and has engaged in an interaction with the profession in a manner that I have not personally experienced from a cabinet minister."

There can be no doubt that Campbell worked assiduously when she served as minister of Justice, spending countless hours on legislation that spanned the gamut of human circumstance. However, despite her dedication, her record of accomplishment is mixed. She deserves credit for designing the "no means no" rape law but should be criticized for her compromise on abortion, for not fighting against the elimination of the Court Challenges Program, for dragging her heels on the Milgaard case and for her reluctance to compensate the victims of brainwashing. She made an extraordinary effort to bring about effective gun control, overcoming enormous resistance from the caucus. Perhaps she cannot be blamed very much for failing to succeed with legislation pertaining to gay rights; after all, even Brian Mulroney was unable to persuade right-wing Tories to vote in favor of ending discrimination against homosexuals.

In the end, the prime minister was pleased with Campbell's performance as Justice minister.

7

BYTOWN BLUES

Every political woman needs to develop skin as tough as
rhinoceros hide.

—*Eleanor Roosevelt*

The cool exterior that Kim Campbell presented at the cabinet
table belied the turbulence of her emotional life. Unlike her
mother's idyllic second marriage, Campbell's union with Howard
Eddy was on the rocks. Her husband's willingness to move to Ottawa
had been a crucial factor influencing her to run in the 1988 election.
She had boasted that having a daily life together was so central to
their marriage that they had decided against the long-distance relationship that many western MPs have with their partners.

At the beginning of their marriage, the couple had enjoyed
weekends of sailing, singing and fine dining. In the summer
months they vacationed aboard the *Western Yew* and at Eddy's
family cottage on Mayne Island, near Vancouver. But the move
to Ottawa disturbed the balance of their life together: they were

deprived of their romantic times at sea and Campbell's work became more demanding.

The spouses of cabinet ministers seem to accept the reality that their husbands or wives will have very little time for them. On the Hill, workdays are long and evenings are often devoted to political events. Weekends are usually taken up with one conference or another. Spouses who move to Ottawa can expect to be dragged to dinners at which people are obsessed with politics, bureaucratic intrigue and Hill gossip. Howard Eddy did not fit into this world. A painfully shy man, he did not enjoy accompanying his wife to dinner parties where he was expected to chat. His discomfort at these occasions was evident and he earned a reputation for being a poor partner at a table. The wife of one Supreme Court justice, who found herself seated beside Eddy at a dinner, later complained to her husband that he was a "bore."

A confidant of Eddy's says that when Howard married Kim, he "thought he was marrying a woman who was going to give him a lot of attention and a lot of her time." Although Campbell did dote on him for a while, as soon as she was appointed to cabinet, her focus changed. The perks of power, the media limelight and the opportunity to put ideas into action galvanized her spirit and energy. She became increasingly occupied with her life on the Hill.

Friends of the couple say that Campbell seemed to be totally absorbed in her career after she became minister of Justice. They remember going out to dinner with Eddy and Campbell and listening to her talk about her career all evening. Even in a family crisis, politics was her first priority. When Eddy had an eye operation and could not see, Campbell left him alone in their apartment while she flew to Vancouver to attend an event in her riding. One of Eddy's children had to take care of him.

Although Campbell has said she was an attentive stepmother, she did not have a lot of time to spend with Eddy's three children, Jonathan and David, who were in their early twenties, and Abby, who was a teenager. One close family friend thinks that Campbell's inattention to his offspring must have been a profound disappointment for Eddy, since re-establishing contact with them was one of the reasons he wanted to move to Ottawa. David, an intellectual like his dad, was the only one with whom Campbell had any rapport. She saw little of Abby and had no contact at all with Jonathan, a very religious young man who detested her for her stand on abortion.

At Christmas, Campbell did not buy her stepchildren individual gifts; nor did she ever treat them to lunch at the Parliamentary Restaurant or take them on a tour of the government buildings. David and Abby were invited to Parliament Hill only once, in 1988, on the day that Campbell was sworn in as an MP. "When she saw the children it was mostly when it was Howard's turn to have them for a holiday or if Howard had them for dinner and they would go out for a Chinese dinner or something like that," says a friend.

One of Eddy's friends thinks that although Eddy had encouraged his wife to reach for the top, he could not tolerate either her great success or her strong commitment to her work. "Although he may have said he was quite happy to share a life and career, I don't think in the long run emotionally this is how he felt," says the friend. "When it comes right down to it, he likes to be number one and it's fine for women to do their own thing as long as doing their own thing doesn't conflict with when he's home, when he wants to go on a holiday with the wife. It's just a case of a man being torn between the basic emotions of what he really wants out of a marriage and what he really wants from a woman but yet trying to espouse the liberal point of view."

In early 1991, after five years of marriage, Eddy walked out on Campbell as suddenly as he had abandoned his first wife. On March 17, a week after Campbell's forty-fourth birthday, he packed his bags and closed the door on their life together. Campbell was devastated when she read his goodbye note and saw the empty closets. She was so caught up in her own world that she hadn't seen it coming. "I had a husband who was quite interested in moving to Ottawa, who had lived there before and his children by his first marriage were there," she said, discussing the break-up with broadcaster Micki Moore in May 1992. "He decided he didn't want to be a political spouse and we separated over a year ago. But I thought I had the problem worked out." They eventually divorced.

Campbell's mother, Lissa, believes Eddy left because he was jealous of her daughter's achievements. Her father, George, thinks the relationship wasn't able to survive Kim's demanding schedule. "As soon as you become a minister the time demands are dreadful, particularly if you're conscientious," he says.

The end of her relationship with Eddy convinced her that she could not combine marriage and a political career again. "The one thing I would not do in public life is marry," she told Peter C. Newman. "I wouldn't impose it on somebody; I wouldn't do it to anybody I care about." However, this pledge did not mean that she had sworn off men.

There was also gossip about a fling with John Tait, the deputy minister of Justice. *Frank*, a satirical magazine that revels in humor and rumor, broadly hinted that Campbell was having an affair with Tait, a married man. The rumors were untrue. "They're completely unfounded. Talking about it but not daring to say it, that I'd had a relationship with my former deputy at Justice. It is absolutely false," she told Heather Bird of *The Ottawa Sun* in May 1993. Campbell suspects the story started after she began taking long walks to lose weight accompanied by Tait, who would brief her.

Campbell has always been willing to discuss her troubled childhood and failed marriages with an openness that many find refreshing. "As far as I'm concerned, if I can't be who I am, it's not worth the candle," she told Graham Fraser of *The Globe and Mail* in December 1992. "I'm not prepared to submerge my own identity. I believe in truth in advertising. Here's who I am. I'm much too lazy to tie myself in knots."

In November 1992, she put her candor to effective use in a moving speech that focussed on the emotional cost of public life. At a conference on women and the media, sponsored by the Canadian Association of Journalists, Campbell used an article by Rosemary Speirs, Ottawa bureau chief for *The Toronto Star*, to argue that women in politics are treated unfairly by the media. Speirs, an ardent feminist, had written that Campbell was "crushingly ambitious," a phrase that Campbell claimed would never be used to describe a male politician. Harking back to the Gillian Shaw article, Campbell complained that some of the "nastiest things" that have ever been written about her were penned by women journalists.

"A recent column in *The Toronto Star*, which I didn't see, but my chief of staff saw, by a woman journalist, described me as 'crushingly ambitious.' What is 'crushingly ambitious'?" she asked the room full of journalists. "I find it extraordinary, because in the course of my life in Ottawa my marriage has ended and I'm very far from home. I find life here often unspeakably lonely and very difficult. And I find that at times of my life when I have been thinking very seriously about whether I wanted to continue to do this, that any success I had in my job is construed as ambitious." She pointed out that her male colleagues have rarely been described with that adjective: "Some of them have explicitly expressed an interest over the years in leading our party, for example, but I never heard that word used in the context of a male. What is it about a woman's success or a woman's aspirations that triggers that term? It reminds me of the old definitions we used to circulate at law school about how a man is forceful, a woman is pushy. A man stands his ground, a woman is a complaining bitch. . . . We cannot encourage women to participate and then punish them for their successes, for the effrontery of aspiring to do more."

Campbell's speech contrasted sharply with the ones delivered by Mary Clancy and Audrey McLaughlin, who praised female journalists and related unpleasant experiences with male scribes. McLaughlin said the "presence of women in journalism has changed what gets reported on the political agenda" because women journalists are "less bound by stereotypes." Clancy said that the "biggest difference between women and men journalists is that women tend to take women politicians and their agendas more seriously."

Campbell's talk received a great deal of favorable publicity and was arguably the most memorable event of the whole conference. Clancy and McLaughlin seemed a bit miffed at being upstaged. McLaughlin remarked that her life had been harder than Campbell's and Clancy expressed her doubts about using the word "lonely" to describe a woman's political career. In Clancy's view, women politicians survive politics much better than men do because women form close networks that offer emotional support. "Most of us will say, 'No, we are not suffering and having these problems,'" she said. Clancy added that she suspected Campbell's speech had been "calculated" to win support among female journalists who would be covering the race for the Conservative leadership.

At the time of Campbell's speech, Brian Mulroney had not yet announced his retirement from politics. However, the minister of Justice had already begun to assemble a team to help her campaign for the leadership in case the prime minister departed. Campbell's criticism of Speirs seemed ill-conceived to some observers, who disagreed that male politicians were never described as ambitious. They argued that serious cabinet ministers were often described in articles as ambitious and noted that John Sawatsky had just published a biography of the prime minister entitled *Mulroney: The Politics of Ambition*. Members of the parliamentary press gallery feel that Campbell was thin-skinned during her stint as minister of Justice. They maintain that no senior minister in Mulroney's second term had such favorable coverage. Yet Campbell seemed to feel that she was often portrayed unfairly in the media. Perhaps this is the reason she made special efforts to influence the media by inviting reporters who were assigned to the justice beat to her office for informal meetings.

Besides these regular, on-the-record meetings, Campbell would sometimes stage social functions with her press coverage in mind. When she invited the justice reporters over to her office for drinks in December of 1992, they arrived just in time to see her playing Christmas carols on an electric piano while Ray Castelli, her chief of staff, smiled in the background. It was obvious that she wanted the journalists to get the impression that she was popular with her employees, says one observer. Reporters who attended the gathering felt that Campbell was trying to butter them up. "We were ushered into her office and we sat around the table and chatted," recalls one journalist. "She was very nice and she was just talking in general terms of what she was up to and she was praising the justice reporters."

Another time, Campbell used a dinner party to reward a reporter whose commentary had pleased her. The incident occurred when Stephen Bindman of Southam News invited her to La Strada, a swank Italian restaurant, for a festive send-off with all the justice reporters before she started her new job as minister of Defence. Campbell's staff requested that they be allowed to review the list of journalists who would be asked to attend the dinner. When the list was returned to Bindman, Cristin Smitz, Ottawa correspondent for *The Lawyer's Weekly*, had been disinvited; her place was taken by *The Globe and Mail's* Graham Fraser, who had recently praised Campbell in a feature. Smitz believes her name was stricken from the list because she had never courted the minister's favor. "My newspaper is very small and I never had a tremendous rapport," she says. "I mean, I never asked any nice questions. I wasn't following her around." Bindman says it was "embarrassing and stupid" to strike Smitz from the invitation list in favor of Fraser, who did not cover justice issues.

Claire Hoy, the acerbic freelance columnist, accuses female journalists and justice reporters of acting like "cheerleaders" for Campbell. He points to the Women and the Media conference as an example of the uncritical devotion she often received. "She got a big ovation from a roomful of journalists for saying women have to stick together. Can you imagine what would happen if a group of men did that?" he asks. Hoy describes the justice reporters as being "all nice and sweet" to her. Bill Rodgers, reporter for CFTO TV and former president of the parliamentary press gallery, agrees: "All you had to do was watch the way the justice reporters would cosy up to her when Kim was being scrummed. It was all contracted in a very chummy, first-name basis tone."

David Vienneau of *The Toronto Star* concurs that Campbell received positive coverage as Justice minister. Although he notes that there were critical articles when the gun control bill was sidetracked, he recalls that for the most part reporters praised her. Bindman says Campbell received "generally favorable" treatment from the press because she was an activist minister: "In terms of volume she got a lot of media coverage. She did way more than previous Justice ministers did."

Even though there were very few negative articles about her, Campbell would easily fly into a temper when she was faced with criticism. Bindman recalls that she became very angry when they appeared together on CBC's "Newsworld" to discuss amendments to the Canadian Human Rights Act. "She was first and then she went into the little room to watch me, and among the things I said was, 'No, this would never become law and yes, Kim Campbell had gone further than any previous Justice minister, but given the timing of the election it won't pass.' The microphone wasn't off for two seconds and I thought she was going to throttle me. She said, 'How could you say that? I never worked so hard. I can't believe you said that. I can't believe you stabbed me in the back like that.' It continued for probably 20 to 25 minutes down the elevator and on the steps outside the press building. She was really furious."

Like Bindman, Peter O'Neil of *The Vancouver Sun* also discovered how easy it was to rouse Campbell's anger. Early in her term as minister of Justice, when she was having difficulty with the gun control bill, O'Neil rated her "B" on a report card that evaluated the performance of B.C. cabinet ministers and MPs. When the bill was finally passed, Campbell glared at O'Neil in a scrum. "She shouted out to me, 'I hope you have feathers in your mouth, Peter, because you said I couldn't do this.' I wouldn't say she was hostile but she was very defiant, with an I-told-you-so attitude." Later, in a private conversation, Campbell berated O'Neil, telling him that he should have been more understanding given the stress she was under because of the break-up of her marriage.

Even Jeffrey Simpson, whose columns in *The Globe and Mail* are generally pleasing to government officials, managed to bruise Campbell's sensitivities by praising her with insufficient enthusiasm. After hearing her speak a number of times, Simpson wrote that Campbell could be prime minister. Although most politicians would have been delighted, Campbell quarrelled with his description of her as "aloof." "I don't know if you've ever noticed, but they [Simpson's compliments] are always grudging," she complained to Trevor Lautens of *The Vancouver Sun*. "He's never heard me speak, and he's never been at a public event with me. So when he writes that I'm aloof, it drives me nuts. I am not an aloof politician. . . . People like me. They call me by my first name. I like it. They like it."

Journalists were not the only targets of Campbell's anger. Milt Harris, head of the Canadian Jewish Congress's Committee on War Crimes, felt her rage in June 1991. The CJC had informed the media that Harris would be in Ottawa to meet with Campbell about the government's slow response in prosecuting Nazi war criminals living in Canada. Unknown to Harris, the minister did not want their meeting covered by the media. Informed that a reporter was outside the room, Campbell became furious, cancelled the meeting and scolded Harris and the other CJC officials.

When Mulroney saw the newspaper coverage about the dispute the next day, he immediately phoned Harris at his home. "He wasn't happy when he phoned me," Harris recalls. Campbell agreed to meet him without the media ten days later. Although she never apologized for her behavior, Harris found her to be very co-operative after the incident, particularly when she realized he was a friend of the prime minister's. "By the time she left the portfolio, I was extremely sorry to see her go," he says, "and I wrote her a note to that effect."

It is also rumored that Campbell can be confrontational with her colleagues in cabinet. One cabinet minister told journalist Robert Russo that she could be "pretty nasty" when she lost battles at the table, and Joe Clark is said to have complained during the 1992 constitutional negotiations that she was constantly meddling in the talks he was brokering. On the other hand, Health Minister Benoît Bouchard and former minister of communications Marcel Masse maintain that Campbell was never nasty. Bouchard says that "Kim could be very emotional and very tough, but never that [nasty], no." Masse describes her as well briefed and willing to take issue with ministers on subjects not within her portfolio.

During her tenure as minister of Justice, Campbell's penchant for making unconventional remarks sometimes caused a stir. In an exchange with burly NDP MP Jim Fulton, Campbell said that the Tories would not be too keen if he crossed the floor. However, she indicated that Nelson Riis, the handsome deputy leader of the NDP, would be welcome. "We kind of like that cute blond-haired guy in the front row," she said to loud hoots. Immediately, she was branded a sexist. "Her true colors are showing. She's not a feminist at all. She's a man in woman's clothing," said New Democrat Lynn Hunter. "If any man had ever said anything like that, you can imagine the barking and growling that would have gone on." Fulton appeared to be the only MP with a sense of humor about the remark. "I was extremely insulted that she would choose Nelson Riis over me," he joked.

Nearly a year later, Campbell captured headlines by casting aspersions on the national anthem. She said that the word "sons" should be changed to "children" in the line "true patriot love in all thy sons command" so that the lyric would not be sexist. Although editorial writers were irked by this suggestion, they became truly incensed when she commented that "O Canada" is not as catchy as "The Star-Spangled Banner." "What is happening to this country when the federal minister of Justice sings high praise for 'The Star-Spangled Banner' and dumps all over 'O Canada'?" asked *The Toronto Star*. Eventually Campbell had to backtrack. "I love the national anthem," she explained. "I said I like ours better than the American because it's singable."

By the fall of 1992, Campbell had become an international media star. When photographer Barbara Woodley snapped a picture of Campbell holding up her judicial robes on a hanger in front of her bare shoulders, she accomplished a public relations miracle. Kim Campbell became the name on everyone's lips neither because of her achievements in cabinet nor for her controversial remarks, but rather because, in Woodley's photograph, she appears to be naked (when, in fact, she is wearing a strapless evening gown). Woodley originally wanted to photograph the minister of Justice with her cello for the book *Portraits: Canadian Women in Focus*, a collection of pictures of such famous women as writer Alice Munro, External Affairs Minister Barbara McDougall, high jumper Debbie Brill, synchronized swimmer Caroline Waldo and the late Governor-General Jeanne Sauvé. However, Campbell resisted Woodley's first idea because she had already posed with her instrument for the September 1990 issue of *Chatelaine*. Since Woodley already had a shot of Supreme Court Justice Beverley McLachlin wearing her black robes, she suggested that Campbell hold her robes in front of her on a hanger. Campbell approved of the plan and searched for something to wear. "So I went downstairs, thinking, 'What should I put on? What can I put on that won't look dumb?'" she told *The Globe and Mail*. "I mean, if I'm holding clothes on a hanger, what do I wear behind that won't look stupid? So I called out to her, 'That only works if my shoulders are bare.'" Woodley agreed.

The photograph had hung in Vancouver's Hongkong Bank building for two years before Nancy Baele, visual arts writer for *The Ottawa Citizen*, spotted it in an exhibition of Woodley's work at the National Arts Centre. When the *Citizen* published the picture on the front page of its Saturday edition on October 31, the photo was picked up by wire services and sent across the country and around the world. Lynn Hunter was one of the few MPs who took offence at Campbell's portrait. She called the pose inappropriate and labelled Campbell the "Madonna of Canadian politics." Most MPs found the picture amusing, symbolic or unimportant. "Hey, if you got it, go for it," said Liberal Mary Clancy. Conservative Barbara Greene thought the picture was meaningful for feminists because it portrayed Canada's first female minister of Justice about to don the robes of the traditionally male-dominated justice system. "I'm more concerned with Madonna's book than Kim Campbell's bare shoulders," said Calgary North MP Al Johnson, leader of the Tories' Family Caucus.

In Britain's tabloids Campbell was described as a "bubbly blond" and a "national pin-up." Confusing *hombros*, the Spanish word for shoulders, with *hombres*, the Spanish word for men, a Mexican newspaper wrote that the Canadian minister of Justice had been photographed with naked men. Campbell loved the attention. "I think it's a hoot," she said, shrugging off the comparison with sex goddess Madonna. "The comparison between me and Madonna is the comparison between a strapless evening gown and gownless evening strap," she quipped. "Seriously, the notion that the bare shoulders of a 43-year-old woman are the source of prurient comment or titillation, I mean, I suppose I should be complimented."

Although the publicity did wonders for the sales of her book, Woodley was not as amused as Campbell by the controversy. Her photograph had been taken out of context and belittled, she said. "Comparing her to Madonna to me just shows that people are visually illiterate," said Woodley, who asked newspaper editors to refrain from using the picture until they talked to her. "I asked Kim Campbell to be one of a collection of inspirational Canadian women. And upon seeing . . . the other women in the book and how I photographed those women, she allowed me the creative freedom to photograph her in the way that I wanted to do so. When it's taken out of the book—and taken out of the context in which it belongs—and when it's put in the papers with things like Madonna and pinups underneath it, then I feel that it belittles the photograph." To Woodley, the portrait "shows Campbell's pride, her self-assurance and sense of humor—she understands the picture artistically instead of worrying about image and hidden meaning."

Campbell's bare shoulders were extraordinarily pleasing to Canadians. Pollster Conrad Winn, president of Compas Inc., said that she captured the imagination of Canadians because she is so unlike Mulroney. "As a personality figure Mulroney is in some ways like a charming, well-dressed undertaker, where she is more like a daring college professor," says Winn. Winn thinks that for a fleeting moment Campbell embodied the hopes and aspirations of a public wishing for significant change.

Angus Reid, one the country's most eminent pollsters, believes that the unconventional photograph was the single most important factor in Campbell's rise to prominence. "I am sure that if a year ago I had done a poll and asked Canadians who is Kim Campbell, I suspect 95 percent of Canadians would say, 'I don't know,'" says Reid. The picture defined Campbell as original and daring in the same way that the roses in Trudeau's lapel became such a defining feature of his years in power. "The picture was a page right out of Trudeau. Not that she was trying to be Trudeau, but it was that kind of slightly offbeat, somewhat controversial, eccentric piece of behavior. It certainly helped to define Kim Campbell as a different politician at a time when Canadians have a lot of trouble with many politicians."

Reid thinks that Canadians wanted a more entertaining type of leadership than they had been offered by Brian Mulroney. When Bill Clinton played "Heartbreak Hotel" on his saxophone on the Arsenio Hall show during the U.S. presidential race, his campaign received a major boost. The portrait of her bare shoulders functioned in a similar way for Campbell; it showed she could be fun. (The photograph is now on permanent display at the National Archives.)

The national media fuelled the publicity by churning out fluff pieces on Campbell. Headlines heralded "Campbellmania" and the minister of Justice was surrounded by TV cameras and reporters wherever she went on the Hill. When Brian Mulroney resigned in February 1993, Chris Cobb, media writer for *The Ottawa Citizen*, charged that the "news media has blindly boosted Campbell's leadership chances" and that journalists had been "willing partners" in building up her image.

Peter Desbarats, dean of the graduate school of journalism at the University of Western Ontario, believes that the media was influenced by the Clinton euphoria south of the border. Although he thought this was understandable, he faulted reporters for not being objective in their treatment of Campbell. Instead of being so eager to depict her as brilliant, talented and interesting, Desbarats thought that reporters should have been more sceptical. For example, he pointed out that news reports asserted she was fluently trilingual, even though no one had bothered to determine just how well she could speak Russian, the language of a country she last visited 20 years ago.

Not until after Campbell declared her candidacy did journalists begin to investigate her life. *Maclean's* magazine and several newspapers assigned reporters to write extensive articles about her family, her work, her politics, her marriages and her divorces. After enjoying incredible adoration in the press, Campbell now complained about the scrutiny of her family's history. "I don't know why the details of my parents' lives or their marriage is anybody's business," she told *The Ottawa Sun*. "They didn't choose public life. I did and I think there's a fundamental ethic there. I'm prepared to answer for myself, but I don't see why . . . they should see the details of their lives discussed for the titillation of people who have never met them."

Campbell should not have blamed the media for probing her family's past. After all, her parents, friends and relatives were speaking to the press of their own free will. Campbell's office actually arranged interviews with her father and gave reporters a list of people who would relate harmless anecdotes about her childhood. Campbell's mother, Lissa, tended to be reticent with journalists, yet she picked a few to hear her version of events. All Campbell had to do was ask her parents not to speak to the media if they did not want their lives exposed.

8

ON THE DEFENCE

Who needs a leadership race? I'll just stage a military coup.
Don't mess with me. I have tanks.

—*Kim Campbell, January 19, 1993*

In late December of 1992 Brian Mulroney had fled the snowstorms that whipped Ottawa to take refuge in Palm Beach. Everyone imagined that the most hated prime minister in the history of Canadian polling had withdrawn to the $3-million waterfront mansion of Florida businessman Charles (Buddy) Jenkins, Jr., to ponder a fateful decision: should he depart the stage with two majority governments to his credit or gamble on winning a third mandate? His advisers presumed that he was keeping the country in suspense while he waited to see if the opinion polls would shoot miraculously skyward.

The upper echelon of the Tory party did not know that the prime minister, in fact, had long ago decided to exit. He had planned to resign in the fall of 1992, bathed in the glory of a historic national

unity pact. But that was not to be. Canadians had delivered a re-
sounding "no" to the Charlottetown Accord and to Mulroney's vision of a decentralized Canada that would give special status to
Quebec. Fed up with constitutional bickering and angry about a recession that they saw as Tory-induced, the voters were also itching
to say "no" at election time.

Mulroney, however, was as usual planning his strategy carefully.
A devoted Tory, he remembered the humiliation he had felt during the many years of Liberal omnipotence. He remembered John
Diefenbaker's ignominious exit from the party leadership. Now he
was determined to leave his party a lasting legacy. He wanted the
Tories to replace the Grits as the natural governing party in the
imagination of Canadians. His plan was to pass the leadership
smoothly to a worthy successor, thereby ensuring a Tory win in
the upcoming election.

One of the secrets of Liberal longevity, he knew, was the party's
ability to hug the centre of the political spectrum while alternat-
ing between leaders from Quebec and English Canada. He viewed
Kim Campbell as the perfect choice for his successor. She was a
westerner, she was very smart and, most important, she was female. (The prime minister is proud to have appointed more
women to cabinet, to senior positions in the bureaucracy and to
the courts than any of his predecessors.) Furthermore, Campbell
was both a popular Justice minister and the darling of the media,
which presented her to the nation as the one Tory capable of
beating Jean Chrétien.

Upon his return from Florida, Mulroney caught the parliamentary press gallery off guard on January 3, 1993, with a surprise
cabinet shuffle. He retired five members, elevated one Quebec
backbencher and shuffled nine ministers to new posts. Campbell's
new assignment was another first in her ground-breaking career.
She became Canada's first—and NATO's only—female Defence
minister. She also picked up responsibility for Veterans Affairs,

was named to the all-powerful Operations Committee and was appointed vice-chair of the cabinet's Committee on Foreign and Defence Policy.

A few observers who thought that Mulroney was punishing Campbell for being too eager to replace him interpreted her switch from the high-profile Justice portfolio to Defence as a step backward. While it is true that in times of peace the minister of Justice has greater prestige than the minister of Defence, Mulroney had moved Campbell to reward her. The Defence portfolio would free her from dealing with gay rights and gun control—issues that irked rural Tory delegates whose support she would need to become the next leader. As Canada's military czar, Campbell could talk tough and show the party her Conservative mettle.

In her new position, Campbell would gain both valuable foreign policy experience and command of a larger budget: in the Justice department she managed a mere $442 million, while Defence and Veterans Affairs have a combined budget of $14 billion. An added bonus of running two departments would be the luxury of having a double political staff—a most useful asset in a leadership race. And, as minister of Defence, Campbell could be photographed in less rarified settings, such as sitting in the cockpit of an F-18 or glad-handing at Legion halls across the country.

Delighted with her new appointment, Campbell rebuffed critics who saw the move as a demotion. "This discussion about the prime minister trying to clip my wings is so off the mark," she said. In a moment of unabashed humor, she admitted to *Maclean's* that she was "flabbergasted" when Mulroney informed her about the new post: "When he told me, I probably said, 'Holy Cow, Prime Minister. Leaping Lizards, Daddy Warbucks.' He was just as pleased as punch with himself."

The opposition parties were as gleeful as Campbell about her appointment. The minister of Defence was now an open target that they planned to attack loudly and often, particularly as she was quickly becoming a leadership hopeful. She inherited the government's expensive plan to purchase submarine-hunting helicopters at a cost of $4.4 billion ($5.8 billion once inflation is taken into account)—a gift to an opposition determined to shoot down the high-flying Campbell.

The new helicopters were faster, more powerful and capable of flying longer distances than Canada's present ageing aircraft. But they appeared to be excessively expensive. The helicopter deal was also redolent of the influence of Brian's friends in high places. Fred Doucet, Mulroney's old friend and former chief of staff, was the key lobbyist for Montreal-based Paramax Systems Ltd., one of the main Canadian companies involved in the EH-101 helicopter deal. In addition, when Paul Manson, head of Paramax and former commander of the Canadian Forces, wanted public relations advice he hired Ian Anderson, a former deputy principal secretary to Mulroney. And when the deal showed signs of unravelling in 1992, Defence Minister Marcel Masse turned to Tory insider Paul Curley, who offered tips on communications strategy for a $50,000 fee. Curley was ideally placed, having purchased a Toronto consulting firm, Advance Planning and Communications, from Hugh Segal, who had been lured to Ottawa to serve as Mulroney's chief of staff. Murray Dobbin argued in *The Canadian Forum* that securing political support in Quebec "means securing the support of business in Quebec and business wants the helicopters."

Suspicions about the plan were also aroused when the government rushed to sign subcontracts for the helicopter, which would make it more difficult for the Liberals to cancel the program if they were elected. Multi-million-dollar contracts were signed in late March, a date that Supply and Services Minister Paul Dick admitted would impose heavy financial penalties on any administration that tried to pull out of the deal. Buzz Nixon, a former deputy minister of Defence, estimated the cost of cancellation at $1.7 billion. "The government has contracts with prime contractors who have agreements with subcontractors all over 12 years—it could be a real whack of cash if anyone wants out," he told *The Winnipeg Free Press*.

Thirty-five of the high-tech machines were ordered in July 1992 from EH Industries Ltd., an Anglo-Italian company, to re-place navy Sea Kings aboard new patrol frigates. Another 15 were purchased to replace the fleet of elderly Labradors used by the Coast Guard for search-and-rescue missions.

Critics assert that the state-of-the art choppers, designed to hunt Soviet submarines, are unnecessary now that the cold war is over. William Kaufmann, a defence analyst at the Brookings Institute in Washington, D.C., notes that most of the submarines from the former Soviet Union are docked in Russian ports. "They're really not out on patrol very much at all. I don't see [any threat], unless you're looking forward into the twenty-first century and a revival of Russian imperialism," he told Geoffrey York of *The Globe and Mail*. Some experts are also convinced that the downwash from the powerful aircraft would be a liability in rescue operations: anyone floating in the sea would probably be drowned by the waves churned up, and anyone waiting on a mountainside would likely be blown off by the winds from the rotors.

Tariq Rauf, a senior researcher at the Canadian Centre for Global Security, argues that the sophisticated EH-101s are far too expensive. He suggests that the government buy smaller, less elaborate helicopters to maintain coastal security and to aid in peacekeeping abroad. Since the government is already spending $1 billion to buy 100 Bell 412 helicopters, Rauf says that these aircraft should be reconfigured for rescue missions. The navy could then purchase off-the-shelf helicopters, such as the French-built Super Puma or the Sikorsky SH-60 Sea Hawk. In addition to Rauf's ideas, Boeing Canada offered another option: it would refit the Labradors for $165 million.

Initially, Campbell was as unsure of the utility of the magnifi-cent flying machines as the critics. In early February, she admitted that she had once had misgivings about the need for such sophisticated aircraft. "I, the innocent minister of Justice at the time, posed the question about the helicopters," she explained. "I was persuaded that it was a good policy, but also the cost of cancelling would be unacceptable. . . . I have a much deeper understanding of where the helicopters fit in in our overall defence priorities."

The burden of defending the purchase of the aircraft in daily parliamentary jousts with the opposition fell on Campbell. She argued effectively that in choppy coastal waters the helicopters would serve as the eyes of the navy patrol frigates and upgraded Tribal class destroyers. "To have frigates without shipboard helicopters is like having an aircraft carrier without aircraft," she told the Commons. "You can't stop halfway through, you can't build the car and say, 'Sorry, we can't afford to put wheels on it.'" Replacing the EH-101 with the Super Puma or Sea Hawk made little sense, she said, because the smaller machines lack sufficient range and power for Canada's military needs.

She dismissed the suggestion to refit the 31 Sea Kings and 13 Labradors as a waste of money and a disservice to the country. The refit would cost $2.5 billion and extend the lives of the machines for only ten years. After that, the navy would still need new aircraft. "After an additional ten years of life, after you have spent $2.5 billion on the helicopters," she told MPs, "you still have to replace them. You still have people flying in 50-year-old airplanes."

Campbell's argument against buying helicopters off the shelf was compelling: she reminded the House of a longstanding practice of using major capital purchases to benefit the domestic economy. According to Campbell, the contract negotiated by the government would create 45,000 jobs: "One of the things that is so important about this project is that $3.2 billion of industrial benefits come to Canada, 45,000 person-years of employment."

Although she did not explain why the country needed a sophisticated anti-submarine helicopter at the end of the cold war,

Campbell handled the opposition adroitly. Liberal MPs complained privately that they were giving her too much exposure on national TV by hounding her about the purchase.

Nevertheless, on April 9, Campbell wavered in her strong public support of the EH-101. During a Tory luncheon speech in Sarnia, Ontario, she hinted that, as prime minister, she might not buy all 50 helicopters. "I don't see with the search-and-rescue helicopters that we could do with fewer," she said. ". . . [But] we might want to review how many we are purchasing for the navy." Her remarks caused consternation in the boardrooms of Mulroney's friends and bolstered the hopes of opponents of the EH-101. "This could be the beginning of efforts by Kim Campbell to distance herself from Brian Mulroney and the decisions associated with him," said NDP defence critic John Brewin.

It was wishful thinking. Campbell was soon back onside, praising the new helicopters. The Montreal *Gazette* stated in an April 30 editorial that "the helicopter order has every appearance of being a make-work project for members of the Tories' old boy network." Other critics think that Campbell's support of the deal shows that she lacks conviction. Even though she knew the purchase was questionable, she became one of its strongest defenders. Some say that at the very least, she could have promised to cut the helicopter order in half to show that she was serious about doing politics differently. Certainly, she did not use the opportunity to distance herself from Mulroney and his friends, some of whom jumped aboard the bandwagon of her campaign.

The Liberals, however, did not distinguish themselves in the debate about the helicopters or use it to their political advantage. Instead of offering a viable alternative to the Tories' plan, they were far more interested in slinging mud at Campbell. In April, when Robert d'Allessandro, the Italian president of the EH-101 consortium, was charged with accepting a $1.6-million kickback on the sale of nine helicopters to the Italian police, the Liberals suggested that the Tory government had also paid kickbacks. They howled for a probe even though there was not a shred of evidence linking Canada to the Italian scandal. Campbell called the Liberals' groundless accusation "one of the shoddier examples of political rhetoric that I've seen during my life in politics."

Although they opposed purchasing the EH-101s, the Liberals did agree that new shipborne helicopters were needed to replace the Sea Kings and Labradors. In the short term, the party favored refitting both types of aircraft until a decision could be reached about suitable replacements. However, as Campbell had pointed out, this plan would not result in real savings. Not only would it be necessary to spend $2.5 billion to refit the Sea Kings and Labradors but an additional $4.5 billion would be required to replace them a decade later. According to government figures, when inflation was taken into account, the Liberal plan would cost taxpayers $8.9 billion, $3.1 billion more than the Tories' program.

Besides failing to come up with a better plan, the Liberals avoided open discussion of the merits of the EH-101. In an unguarded moment, Liberal MP Fred Mifflin, a retired admiral, admitted to a Commons committee in mid-May: "The best helicopter is probably the EH-101 . . . that is certainly an excellent helicopter." Mifflin flew into a rage outside the Commons when his remark was reported by Bill Rodgers of CFTO News. "Do you realize what Kim Campbell could do with this?" he hollered at Rodgers.

As frontrunner for the Tory leadership, Campbell expected to face intense scrutiny over matters like the helicopter purchase. Nevertheless, when she accepted her new job, she could not have anticipated that she would be involved in a controversy about military operations abroad. Since Canadian soldiers who serve in trouble spots around the world generally win rave reviews for being restrained and highly disciplined, the minister of Defence usually basks in the glory of successful peacekeeping missions. Campbell, however, had the bad luck of holding the Defence portfolio when the image of the Canadian forces fell under a dark cloud.

The trouble began four months after 900 crack paratroopers from the elite Canadian Airborne Regiment arrived in Somalia. The combat-ready brigade had been dispatched to the East African country in December as part of a U.S.-led operation to maintain peace among warring clans and to protect supplies for famine relief. "Operation Deliverance" was looking like another public relations coup for the military until four Somalis ended up dead at the hands of Canadian troops.

One tragic incident occurred on February 17, 1993, in Belet Huen, 160 miles north of the capital of Mogadishu, when one Somali was killed and three wounded after an officer ordered his troops to fire on a crowd of protesters who were throwing rocks. A second man died and another was wounded on March 4, when soldiers shot at two unarmed Somalis trying to climb through razor wire surrounding the base. When Canadians were first informed of the incident, the military described the Somalis as suspected saboteurs and insisted that warnings had been given before the soldiers fired. Several weeks later, the country heard a different version of the event. In a letter made public by his wife, Maj. Barry Armstrong, a military doctor, charged that the dead Somali had been murdered in cold blood. Armstrong alleged that the victim was first shot in the back while he was running away and then shot in the head and neck after he had fallen.

On March 16, another Somali was killed. He had been caught sneaking into the Canadian compound, and died after receiving a beating. Although five soldiers were arrested in connection with this incident, the Canadian public was not informed until two weeks later. The military acknowledged that the death was being treated as a homicide only after an enterprising reporter for *The Pembroke Observer* revealed that one of the soldiers accused of beating the Somali had tried to hang himself in jail.

Just one day after the beating, a Somali Red Cross worker became the fourth man to die. He was shot by Canadian troops after he allegedly fired at a crowd and threatened paratroopers who were trying to distribute food.

In late March and April 1993, when the incidents were revealed in the House, Campbell was out of Ottawa campaigning for the leadership. Knowing that she was distracted from her portfolio, opposition MPs moved in for the attack. "It's about time that we had a minister of Defence in place who has the capacity, the interest and the time to deal with the serious problems affecting us in Somalia," Liberal foreign affairs critic Lloyd Axworthy told the Commons on April 23.

The task of defending the Defence department's response to the killings fell to Government House Leader Harvie Andre. His efforts to cool the furor in the Commons were futile. It was apparent that there had been a cover-up, and the opposition was concerned that the soldiers responsible for the deaths might escape justice. In late April, Campbell rushed home from a campaign tour of the Maritimes to deal with the growing parliamentary crisis. After a long delay, two teams of military investigators had been dispatched to delve into the events of March 4 and 16. But Campbell was determined to show that she was in control as Defence minister. Three days after her return to Ottawa, she ordered a special military board of inquiry into the killings.

Critics said that Campbell was running for cover. The inquiry would be held in secret and would not deal with the criminal aspects of the March incidents. (Four soldiers were later charged for the beating death.) Significantly, the report of the military board would not be published until July, when the Conservative leadership race was over and Canadians were on vacation. Lewis MacKenzie, a retired general who won fame for his peacekeeping efforts in the Balkans, thought the investigation had been designed to provide a smokescreen for Campbell. "I don't think that it has to be held from the point of view of the preparation of the unit," he said. "But I think it has to be held from the point of view of a person who is deep in the middle of a political battle and has to find some way to deflect or delay."

In early May, before she could catch her breath from responding to the killings in Somalia, Campbell was forced to deal with yet another scandal. CBC's "Prime Time News" reported that Cpl. Matt McKay, a member of the airborne regiment in Somalia, had been involved with neo-Nazis while stationed in Winnipeg in 1990. McKay, who claimed to have since renounced his affiliation with the racist group, was photographed wearing a Hitler T-shirt, standing in front of a swastika. In addition, another soldier who had formerly served in the airborne admitted to training recruits for the Church of the Creator, a cell of the Ku Klux Klan.

While both the B'nai Brith and the Canadian Jewish Congress called for federal inquiries into the allegations, opposition MPs seemed to care more about destroying Campbell's credibility than rooting out racists in the military. Because the minister of Defence was absent from the Commons when the allegations were reported, the opposition could accuse her of being asleep at the switch. Deputy NDP Leader Nelson Riis suggested that she had lost control of her department. "You have to wonder how up to date or how informed the minister is in terms of what's going on in her department," he told the Commons on May 7.

In contrast to her reaction to the murders in Somalia, Campbell was quick to respond to this crisis created by the opposition. Within days of the CBC allegations, she promised new rules for screening out members of racist groups from the military. "We have not, to date, in our recruiting, deliberately asked people about their memberships," she told MPs. "I am instituting a review of our recruiting policies to ensure that is done." She announced that the board of inquiry she had appointed in April to report on the incidents in Somalia would also investigate racism in the airborne regiment.

Despite opposition attempts to label her as soft on racists, Campbell emerged with her reputation intact.

Campbell was even able to distinguish herself as a strong manager of her new portfolio. When she assumed responsibility for the Ministry of Defence, she said that it would be impossible for her to "separate my perspective of the world as a woman from what I do in any portfolio." Opposition MPs jumped on her words and demanded that she act quickly to eradicate sexual harassment from the armed forces. They had no shortage of evidence to corroborate claims that women were being mistreated in the military. A government report in June 1992 concluded that "sexual harassment is rife" in the Canadian Forces. Max Yalden, head of the Canadian Human Rights Commission, agreed. In his 1992 report to Parliament, Yalden said that widespread hostility toward women makes sexual harassment far more prevalent in the military than in any other segment of society.

Because the Ministry of Defence was already in the process of responding to Yalden's concerns, Campbell had no difficulty giving the issue a swift and impressive response. In the fall of 1992, the Defence department had commissioned a survey of 5,600 staff members to measure the extent of sexual harassment. When the results were released in mid-May, it was revealed that one-quarter of women in the Canadian Forces had experienced harassment. "Obviously this is way too much," Campbell told reporters. To remedy the situation, she announced a sweeping policy that would require all incidents of sexual harassment to be reported to Defence headquarters. "We have now created harassment officers who function outside the chain of command so [the complainants] can have a greater sense of security when they report incidents," she said. She also ordered the department to undertake a military education program for dealing with harassment.

Campbell proved to be adept at fighting fires in her portfolio even though the leadership campaign consumed most of her

time. However, some observers say that she tended to push defence issues aside unless she thought they could yield political
mileage. For example, when Norwegian Defence Minister Johan
Jorgen Holst sought a meeting with her in March on his way back
to Norway after a visit to Washington to talk about the possibility
of locating a United Nations Peacekeeping College in Canada,
Campbell's office said she was too busy to see him. Holst felt that
Canada would be the ideal place to set up the college to train soldiers for peacekeeping; obviously, she did not agree.

A minister of Defence with nearly 20 years of experience,
Holst took offence at Campbell's refusal to meet him. In contrast,
U.S. Defence Secretary Les Aspin, who was recovering from heart
surgery, invited Holst to meet him at his bedside in the hospital.
"It was a diplomatic snub," says a friend of Holst's. "Aspin was in
hospital and he met with Holst in the hospital." Holst decided to
visit Canada anyway, travelling to Toronto after his visit to
Washington. Coincidentally, he was in the city on the same day
that Campbell was there campaigning for the leadership.

It is difficult to evaluate Campbell's performance in Defence because she held the portfolio for only a short time. Furthermore,
she was so busy with the leadership race that important defence
projects such as Canada's peacekeeping efforts in former
Yugoslavia have had to be handled either by External Affairs
Minister Barbara McDougall or by Brian Mulroney himself. As a
part-time minister of Defence, Campbell attended few department
briefings and rarely appeared in the Commons to answer opposition queries. Her infrequent visits to the House left her vulnerable
to attacks by MPs.

Just before Campbell declared herself a candidate for the Tory
leadership, several advisers urged her to withdraw from cabinet.
They suggested that resigning would free her from any obligations to
defend government policy. Had she heeded this counsel, she could
have distanced herself from the helicopter purchase, avoided any

connections with the tragedies in Somalia and given the opposition fewer opportunities to attack her. By choosing to stay in Defence, Campbell suffered the consequence of having her name linked to controversy and scandal. On the other hand, she showed she was capable of handling a difficult portfolio. Given her history of tenacity, it is not surprising that she chose not to take the easy way out.

On balance, defence experts say that Campbell handled her two portfolios very well in the midst of a gruelling leadership campaign. They point out that the Ministry of Defence was better managed under Campbell than it had been under Marcel Masse, who had spent most of his time flying around the world at public expense. Alex Morrison, of the Canadian Institute of Strategic Studies, maintains that Campbell brought a capable ministerial staff to Defence that quickly improved the administration of the department. "The minister herself adapted readily," he says. "And I think, given the little miscues whenever you take over a new job, the impression around Defence headquarters is that she has done very well. They appeared to be very pleased with her."

9

THE HARE AND THE TORTOISE

"And yet," said the Tortoise, "although I have neither your lightness of foot nor the compact and powerful symmetry of your haunches, I will undertake to run you a wager."

—*Aesop's Fables*

Pierre Trudeau haunts Brian Mulroney like Anthony Perkins's mother in Hitchcock's *Psycho*. The working-class kid from Baie-Comeau is always measuring himself against the wealthy aristocrat from Montreal. When Mulroney swept into power in 1984 he hoped to leave a legacy greater than that of his Liberal predecessor. The policies that Trudeau designed to promote Canadian nationalism, strengthen the central government and cultivate a healthy scepticism of Uncle Sam were to be undone. The Mulroney doctrine would be radically different:

less government, a pro-American agenda and a decentralized Canada.

Mulroney succeeded in halting Canada's evolution as a welfare state by making deep cuts in government subsidies and services. He saddled the nation with higher taxes that widened the gap between rich and poor and negotiated free trade pacts with the United States and Mexico. No other prime minister has had a closer relationship with the Americans.

Mulroney's greatest failure was, ironically, seen as Trudeau's greatest accomplishment: he could not convince English Canada that federalism should be adapted to accommodate Quebec. Most voters preferred Trudeau's vision of a strong central government unencumbered by special status for *la belle province*.

Like Trudeau, Mulroney chose the month of February to announce his exit from the political stage. On February 23, 1993, he met with Quebec lieutenant Benoît Bouchard, Senate Speaker Guy Charbonneau, Finance Minister Don Mazankowski and Toronto lawyer Sam Wakim. Among these four political allies, only Charbonneau had known for nearly a year that his old friend intended to step down. A Tory bagman who had raised money to support Mulroney's challenge to Joe Clark's leadership, Charbonneau had kept silent about the prime minister's plans to resign, not even confiding the secret to his wife, Yolande.

The day after Mulroney informed his closest confidants that he would step down in June after a new leader had been chosen, he invited another two dozen of his friends and associates to 24 Sussex Drive to hear the news. He then drove to Parliament Hill to inform his caucus. In a 45-minute speech that was punctuated by eight standing ovations, the prime minister reviewed the accomplishments of his nearly nine years in office: he had been in power longer than 14 prime ministers—only Sir John A. Macdonald, Sir Wilfrid Laurier, Mackenzie King and Pierre Trudeau had stayed longer; he had delivered two majority governments and outlasted 19 provincial premiers. Unlike Trudeau, who had left the Liberals nearly bankrupt when he made his exit, Mulroney had made sure before his departure that the Progressive Conservative Party had a bulging war chest to fight an election. He expressed the hope that he would be remembered more kindly by historians than he was by the Canadian public.

Kim Campbell was way ahead of the other leadership contenders when the bell rang to start the race: she had been preparing to succeed Mulroney since the summer of 1992. To remedy her lack of experience with economic matters, she held brainstorming sessions with academic economists such as Richard Lipsey. Private dinners were arranged for her to meet key Conservatives in Montreal and Toronto.

By Christmas, Campbell had put together an informal organization that was active in several regions of the country. Marcel Masse, the nationalist conscience of the Quebec caucus, shepherded her around Quebec; John Bassett, a millionaire broadcaster, introduced her to Toronto's elite. Out on the West Coast, money was being raised by Canadian National chairman Brian Smith, the former Socred cabinet minister whom Campbell had supported at the 1986 leadership convention after she was eliminated on the first ballot.

News of Campbell's organizing drive sparked furious efforts by other contenders to assemble their own teams to stop her momentum. Trade Minister Michael Wilson, who had planned to leave politics, hit the ground running. Although he was closely identified with the Canada–U.S. free trade deal and the unpopular GST, the former Finance minister had little trouble raising $3 million from the Bay Street financial establishment. Jim Ramsay, Wilson's chief of staff, was seeking-out advertising and communications strategists and had taken a poll to assess Wilson's chances.

Environment Minister Jean Charest moved crackerjack Tory organizer David Small into his office to set up a nationwide campaign. Jean's brother, Robert Charest, began phoning ministers and others to ask for support. Communications Minister Perrin Beatty initiated his campaign by enlisting the aid of lobbyist Bruce McClellan and fundraiser Pieri Mieli. Veteran organizer John Laschinger was tapped to test the waters for Barbara McDougall, minister of External Affairs. Even Joe Clark began to reconsider his decision to leave politics.

Many Conservative MPs were pushing Don Mazankowski and Benoît Bouchard to enter the race as a team. Mazankowski would run for leader with Bouchard acting as his deputy in French Canada in a relationship reminiscent of that between Sir John A. Macdonald and George-Étienne Cartier.

Jockeying for the leadership became so intense that Mulroney felt compelled to issue an edict. At a cabinet meeting in early February he instructed the contenders to stop the wheeling and dealing. No one listened; the scheming continued, albeit quietly and underground.

As frontrunner, Campbell glowed in the days after Mulroney called a leadership convention. A Gallup poll released on February 27 showed that the Conservatives would run neck and neck with the Liberals if she were their leader; the other contenders did not come close to matching her popularity. By mid-March, an Angus Reid poll showed Campbell was favored two to one over Jean Chrétien as the best choice for prime minister. Reid noted that the country wanted to break with the past and that Campbell appeared to represent the biggest change from the Mulroney years. On March 22, a *Maclean's* poll, conducted by Ottawa-based Compas Inc., found that Campbell had the support of the vast majority of Conservatives and could easily sweep to victory at the leadership convention scheduled for June 9–13.

The favorable polls convinced the Tory establishment that Campbell had the royal jelly needed to win the next election. Sensing victory, senior Tories hastened to join Campbell's parade.

When Treasury Board president Gilles Loiselle, a strong nationalist and the Quebec City region political boss, pledged her his support, Justice Minister Pierre Blais, a friend of Charest's, feared that his clout as political boss in eastern Quebec would be usurped. Although his role of campaign co-chair of the Tory election machine obliged him to remain neutral, Blais decided to work for Campbell. In early March he met with 50 Quebec organizers and urged them to back the minister of Defence by suggesting that she was Mulroney's choice. When the prime minister heard about this backroom dealing, he was so furious that he made Blais resign as campaign co-chair.

The majority of the cabinet and caucus went over to Campbell, along with most of the senior players in the backroom. One of Campbell's early supporters was Senator Norman Atkins, who had orchestrated Mulroney's 1984 and 1988 electoral victories as well as several successful campaigns for Bill Davis, the former premier of Ontario. In January 1991, Atkins had arranged for Campbell to speak at the Albany Club's Sir John A. Macdonald dinner so that she could be introduced to powerbrokers in Toronto. Along with Atkins came some remnants of the Big Blue Machine and a coterie of strategists, organizers and political lieutenants, including Paul Curley, Bill Neville, Patrick Kinsella, David Camp, Nancy Jamieson and Alan Schwartz, a Toronto businessman and chief fundraiser.

Quebec nationalist MPs, such as Jean-Pierre Blackburn and Suzanne Duplessis, signed on, as did Don Blenkarn, Benno Friesen and John Reimer, right-wing MPs from B.C. and Ontario. Ideology was not an element in the race; Tories backed Campbell because they saw her as giving them the best chance to hang on to power.

The media played into her campaign with effusive articles and TV profiles. For example, in the March 6 edition of *The Ottawa Citizen*, journalist Julian Beltrame told readers: "Get ready for Campbellmania. Not since Pierre Trudeau exploded on the national scene in 1968 has a rookie politician aroused so much excitement, publicity and, yes, 'hope for change' as the fast-talking blonde from Lotusland."

Peter Desbarats, dean of the graduate program in journalism at the University of Western Ontario, complained that the media was not subjecting Campbell to sufficient scrutiny. "She is a new face, bright, ambitious and quite exciting, at a time when Canadians, who are influenced by what is going on in the United States, are looking for younger leaders," he told *The Vancouver Sun*. "But that doesn't absolve journalists of their responsibility of reporting comprehensively and accurately and reasonably objectively."

At the outset of the leadership race, few newspapers bothered to ask important questions about Campbell's background and policies. *The Vancouver Sun* and *The Globe and Mail* were exceptions. The *Sun*, which was more familiar with the B.C. MP's strengths and weaknesses than papers in other parts of the country, said that it was dismayed that Canadians were so enamored of Campbell when they did not know what she stood for. An editorial in the *Globe* was highly critical of the Tories' eagerness to back her: "The rush of so many Tories to embrace a candidate about whose background, expertise and beliefs they know next to nothing, bespeaks a party that has no real reason to govern . . . What do we know of Kim Campbell?"

The campaigns of Campbell's serious rivals were undercut by the fawning media coverage she was receiving and by the polls that trumpeted her "winnability." When word leaked that Senator Charbonneau, the Tory godfather of Quebec and Mulroney's closest confidant, was raising money for her campaign, Conservatives knew that Campbell was Mulroney's favorite.

Wilson asked Charbonneau if he was backing Campbell. The senator said that although he would raise money for any candidate who asked, his response to Wilson's leadership bid was lukewarm at best; he respected the former Finance minister's intellect but felt he was a "lousy politician." After this conversation, Wilson withdrew from the race. He had already lost one bid for the leadership in 1983, and saw no point in setting himself up for another defeat.

Barbara McDougall and Employment and Immigration Minister Bernard Valcourt bowed out of the contest, as did Perrin Beatty, Revenue Minister Otto Jelinek and Tom Hockin, minister of state for Small Businesses and Tourism. Organizers for Wilson, McDougall and Beatty privately complained that Mulroney had rigged the race in Campbell's favor and fast-tracked her career. They said that the prime minister had turned a blind eye to Campbell's organizing at the same time that he was rapping the knuckles of her rivals as they tried to play catch-up in advance of his resignation announcement. On the day she dropped out of the race, McDougall was bitter about Mulroney's perceived favoritism: Kim Campbell will find out that "getting into bed with Brian Mulroney is like getting into bed with an elephant," she told CTV's Mike Duffy.

By mid-March, the only contenders left to challenge Campbell were Patrick Boyer, a soft-spoken lawyer, and Garth Turner, former business editor of *The Toronto Sun*, both from Ontario. Edmonton Southwest MP Jim Edwards, a former broadcaster, entered the race on March 26 to represent the right wing of the party on economic and social issues, and Guelph foundry owner John Long announced his candidacy on March 31. (Long dropped out in mid-May after the candidates' fifth and final televised debate.)

Mulroney feared that a contest with only one strong candidate would make for a boring leadership race that would hurt the party in two ways: the Conservatives would lose the advantage of three months of media attention and voters would not be convinced that the Tories were engaged in a major renewal. On Mulroney's orders, Chief of Staff Hugh Segal called Don Mazankowski, Tom

Hockin and other ministers to urge them to seek the leadership. Segal's efforts did not meet with success: no one wanted to go through a gruelling campaign just to make choosing a leader look like a horse race.

Even Jean Charest was thinking of abandoning his ambition to be leader. Campbell's lead seemed insurmountable and the minister of the Environment did not want to be humiliated at the convention. He was also worried about money. Not being a wealthy man, the father of three was reluctant to end up deep in debt. When a desperate Mulroney summoned Charest to 24 Sussex Drive to encourage him to seek the leadership "for the good of the party," he promised that Charbonneau would raise money for his campaign. The prime minister told the young Quebecker that the leadership was not necessarily in the bag for Campbell. Should she stumble, Charest would be there to put on the mantle.

Charest hesitated about entering the race, even though his wife, Michèle Dionne, encouraged him. Senator Michael Meighen, a Toronto lawyer and grandson of former prime minister Arthur Meighen, urged him not to run, while Alberta MP Jack Shields was equally adamant that he should. "It's a win-win situation," Shields said. "If you win, you will become prime minister. If you finish second, you've raised your profile." Transport Minister Jean Corbeil, Sports Minister Pierre Cadieux, Quebec businessman George Maclaren, Alberta Premier Ralph Klein and former Saskatchewan premier Grant Devine also offered their support.

A telephone call to Denis Beaudoin, a longtime friend who was working in Rwanda, helped Charest make up his mind. Beaudoin told him to go for the brass ring, as did Amélie, Charest's ten-year-old daughter. "So, Daddy, are you going to do it?" Charest recalled her asking. "Are you going to run for prime minister? Because I think you should."

Charest, a native of Sherbrooke, in Quebec's Eastern Townships, is a natural politician who is fluent in both official languages. As

Clark's township organizer in the 1983 leadership campaign, he had outflanked the forces of Brian Mulroney. The next year, at the age of 26, he won the Tory nomination in Sherbrooke over the candidate favored by the riding association and went on to beat the Liberal incumbent who was expected to trounce him in the 1984 general election. In 1986 he became the youngest cabinet minister in Canadian history when Mulroney appointed him minister of state for Youth. Two years later, he was promoted to the office of Fitness and Amateur Sports, where he faced his first setback: he was forced to resign from cabinet in January 1990 because he had phoned a judge who was handling a case that involved the Canadian Track and Field Association.

This foolish mistake did not damage his relationship with Mulroney, who saw the future of the Conservative party in the boyish Charest. The prime minister appointed him to chair the Commons committee, attempting to forge a compromise to ensure passage of the Meech Lake Accord. Charest's hard work on the committee impressed Mulroney and he soon invited the young man back to the cabinet table to serve as minister of the Environment.

Of course, Charest did not have the same clout as Campbell in the cabinet. Because he did not sit on either the Operations or the Expenditure Review committees, he could not play a major role in the government and was unable to halt the declining influence of his department.

Charest knew he faced enormous odds in his bid to defeat Campbell. Nevertheless, he was determined to turn the fable of the tortoise and the hare into reality. He knitted together a campaign organization, nicknamed "Team Tortoise," that included some of the wisest political pros in the Conservative party. Savvy strategist Jodi White, a former senior aide to Joe Clark, became his campaign manager; David Small was put in charge of operations and Tim Ralfe was responsible for the media. Mulroney stalwarts such as lobbyist Gary Ouellet, Pat MacAdam and Pierre Claude Nolin were recruited for their strategic, communications and organizational skills. All were veterans of leadership contests and none played by the rules laid down by the Marquess of Queensberry. Bright novices, like Heather Conway and pollster Bruce Anderson, rounded out the team.

Charest and his advisers expected Campbell's daunting lead to shrink when the opposition and the media started to focus on her. They hoped that three factors would upset the Campbell juggernaut. First, Charest thought he was a better speaker than his opponent and was confident that he could outperform her in the televised leadership debates. His campaign team insisted that two of the five debates take place before the delegate selection meetings. Campbell's advisers would later regret agreeing to this.

Second, Charest planned to announce policy initiatives before Campbell did. Although his ideas were hardly startling, he was first off the mark with promises to eliminate the deficit, reduce the national debt, cut the size of cabinet, change unemployment insurance and foster a "modern and open" relationship between Quebec and the rest of the country. Since Campbell's popularity was based on being a fresh face, Charest's organizers thought that delegates might become disillusioned if she failed to match her charisma with bold statements about policy. Charest would then come across as the candidate with better ideas.

Third, unlike Charest, Campbell did not have a long history in the Tory party. His years of work for the Conservatives might stand him in good stead with delegates if Campbell's "winnability" started to tarnish.

Campbell's popularity not only spooked her leadership rivals but also worried Liberal MPs, who saw their dreams of unseating the Tories evaporate. Disturbed by the "nervous nellies" in his caucus, Jean Chrétien publicly scolded them for giving in to panic. "People don't vote for crybabies. They vote for people who have confidence in themselves," he told reporters on March 17 as he entered the party's weekly caucus meeting.

Chrétien also charged that Mulroney had bungled the leadership contest from the start by trying to rig the race in Campbell's favor: "Mulroney is trying to undo what he has done. He got Charest in. When a leader wants to leave he doesn't choose his successor. He lets the party decide."

The Liberals launched a relentless attack on the minister of Defence in an effort to slow her momentum. Nearly every day, the front benches of the opposition fired salvos at her in the House of Commons, while researchers pored over her old speeches in a desperate search for dirt. A Chrétien aide purportedly offered to buy the tape of Campbell's 1986 interview with Gillian Shaw. "He offered to pay me for the tape. It was appalling to even discuss," said Shaw. Norman Ruff, a political scientist at the University of Victoria, thought the nasty tactics were outdated: "This is the kind of politics everybody left behind in the 1950s, buried down in an older darker age," he told *The Vancouver Sun*. "It shows just how worried the Chrétien organization is with Campbell's entry into the race."

Unfazed by the Liberal attacks, Campbell set about forming her campaign team. Her major strategists included Patrick Kinsella, a friend from her days in Bill Bennett's office, and cabinet ministers Perrin Beatty, Gilles Loiselle, Pierre Blais, Doug Lewis, Tom Siddon and Senator Lowell Murray. She appointed Newfoundland MP Ross Reid to serve as her campaign manager, and her chief of staff, Ray Castelli, as director of operations. Although Reid had acquired some experience when he ran John Crosbie's failed leadership bid in 1983, he was neither as tough nor as wily as the operators who signed on with Charest.

Reid's greatest mistake was failing to establish a clear chain of command. The organization was top-heavy and slow-moving with nearly 50 directors and countless backroom tacticians who all wanted to exercise their influence. "It was like a commune," said one insider. "It was fun. It was exciting. But nothing was getting done. No decisions were being made."

A few days before Campbell officially declared her candidacy, she set tongues wagging by having country singer George Fox accompany her to the Juno Awards in Toronto. Campbell had chosen "Clearly Canadian," a Fox country tune, as her campaign theme song to counter her image as a cello-playing intellectual. The 33-year-old singer was written into the script by one of Campbell's friends, who asked George if he would interrupt a concert tour in Victoria to escort Kim to the Junos. Although Fox enjoyed himself during the well-publicized evening they spent together, he discovered that Campbell knew very little about country music. He was rebuffed by her staff when he tried to arrange another date.

On March 25, Campbell kicked off her leadership campaign in the ballroom of the Hotel Vancouver. "Why do I want to be prime minister? The answer is not because I want to live at 24 Sussex Drive," Campbell told an audience of 1,000 supporters. "I guess what it boils down to is I'd like to change the way people think about politics in this country by changing the way we do politics." She called for a "politics of inclusion" that would break down barriers between people and government. "In a democracy, government isn't something that a small group of people do *to* everybody else, it's not even something they do *for* everybody else, it should be something they do *with* everybody else."

Campbell was radiant at the event, sparkling with a sense of humor that belied her reputation as an elitist. The crowd roared when she announced that Saskatchewan MP Larry Schneider had said his "raunchy ranchers" really liked her. "That's because they know that under this cool, arrogant, intellectual, urbane exterior . . . there beats the heart of a Texas line dancer." And she was prophetic in predicting that the media would turn on her:

"Somebody asked me in Kitchener . . . why the media loved me and I indicated that whether they did or did not, I wasn't sure I accepted the premise of the question, but it was likely to be a short-lived relationship and I expected to be left at the altar on this one."

Although her speech crackled with catchy phrases and witty one-liners, it was devoid of substantial ideas about the issues that faced the nation. Promising to unveil detailed policies over her three-month campaign, Campbell again declared that her main goal was to close the gap between citizens and government through the "politics of inclusion." Colleagues from her days at the Vancouver School Board thought her packaged image as an "inclusive" politician who would invite everyone to have a hand in policy making was completely out of character. Jonathan Baker, a friend and trustee during Campbell's school-board term, complained that her handlers were hiding the candidate's true nature. "I'm a little bit surprised at this whole thing about the politics of inclusion," Baker fumed. "She should just be herself and fire all the god-damned hacks and flacks and spin doctors. Let Kim be Kim, and that is not Kim."

Campbell's team decided to run a classic frontrunner's campaign that would refrain from laying out any ideas that the opposition could use as a bludgeon. The candidate would not offer distinctive policies to distinguish her from Mulroney, her leadership rivals or the opposition parties. "People don't want to focus on that kind of minutiae," Ross Reid explained defensively. "Canadians don't expect all of the options from politicians. People expect leaders to lead."

Besides instructing her to avoid specifics, Campbell's handlers advised her to dampen her spontaneity. They feared that their candidate's sharp tongue and quick wit could become a liability if her one-liners were misinterpreted. She was to exercise restraint in order to coast to an easy victory.

In early April, the tops of the first crocuses appeared on Parliament Hill along with the first signs of trouble for Campbell's campaign. Energy Minister Bill McKnight, a respected member of the cabinet and a roommate of Don Mazankowski's, was no fan of the minister of Defence. The two had clashed around the cabinet table, and he feared that she would lead the party to defeat at the polls. McKnight arranged a meeting in Toronto with Bernard Valcourt and Michael Wilson to search for another high-profile candidate. The three concluded that the right man for the job was Hugh Segal, a bilingual, smooth communicator with deep roots in the party and a knack for creating policy. "He had a lot to offer and we felt he would make an excellent choice for leader," McKnight explained.

Although Segal had never held elective office and had been associated with more losing than winning leadership campaigns, he agreed to enter the race if three conditions were met: he wanted a credible organization, money to run an effective campaign and the support of some prominent women. The gender of his team was a major concern to Segal because he did not want to be seen as undermining women by challenging the party's first potentially victorious female candidate.

Despite their late start, the trio of McKnight, Valcourt and Wilson had little trouble meeting Segal's first two conditions. Ottawa consultant Harry Near, a consummate political organizer, joined the group along with his business partner Bill Fox, an old chum of Mulroney's, and Jim Ramsay, Wilson's chief of staff. Money came easily: Bill Davis, the former premier of Ontario, and Eddie Goodman, a Toronto lawyer, raised nearly $1 million for Segal in just a few days.

Nevertheless, Segal's campaign for the leadership did not get under way. Barbara McDougall, whom Segal had coached through her cabinet years, refused to endorse him. She still resented Mulroney and his staff for what she believed was the prime minister's clandestine support of Campbell. But the biggest blow to Segal's candidacy came from Mulroney himself, who was in Los Angeles visiting Ronald Reagan when reporters informed him of his top aide's aspiration. He laughed out loud when he heard the news. "Mulroney laughing it off and McDougall's decision not to play were the big issues that turned the tide," says one of Segal's supporters. On April 8, Segal called a news conference to say that he would not be a candidate. Campbell would not have to face a challenge from the party's old guard; however, that Segal had even considered entering the race signified that an important segment of the Tory establishment was unhappy with a Campbell coronation.

Campbell's strategy began to unravel during the first two leadership debates that took place before the delegate selection meetings began on April 22. In the first debate, in Toronto, her performance was stiff compared to that of Charest, who was charming, quick-witted and decisive. At one point candidates were asked for specific ideas on ways to eliminate the deficit. Charest called for a freeze on government spending, fewer federal departments and a smaller cabinet. Campbell refused to discuss any measures to cut the deficit until she had talked to Canadians.

Realizing that she had not done very well in the first debate, Campbell complained that the format was stilted and admitted that "expectations were too high" because of the favorable media coverage she had received. Charest put it best: "Quite frankly, I didn't find there was a lot of substance in what she had to say during the debates."

The arrogance that had been such a part of Campbell's earlier political life began to resurface and added to her troubles. Before a single delegate had been chosen, Campbell talked about calling an early general election. On April 18, during a swing through Quebec, she bragged that she was smarter and more accomplished than Charest, who had been implying that her style betrayed a lack of substance. "One has to admit that I did more in my four years than

Jean Charest did in his eight," she told Radio-Canada. "I managed many difficult dossiers. I resolved dossiers that no one thought I was able to do—firearms, sexual assault. . . . I initiated a process to finally resolve the demands of natives in British Columbia."

Worried by her weak presentation in Toronto and concerned about the media's new inclination to view her negatively, Campbell's strategists rushed to attach some substance to their frontrunner. She put forward 25 proposals for democratic reform of Parliament that included allowing more free votes, permitting MPs to vote from their ridings, studying the need for a new federal ombudsman and considering ways for citizens to force national referenda. Critics pointed out that her ideas were not new and fell short of the suggestions for reform offered by the Liberals and New Democrats. "She's copying me," Jean Chrétien told reporters. "We made those proposals many months ago and the government has done nothing about it."

During the campaign Campbell gradually unveiled a range of rather vague policies. For example, she pledged to wipe out the deficit in five years but supplied no details about how to do it. She suggested a major review of the management and delivery of health care and hinted that wealthy Canadians would have their old age pensions cut, but provided no specifics. Although Campbell talked a lot about promoting small business and expanding trade to the Pacific Rim, her ideas on these subjects were neither clear nor novel.

In Montreal on April 21, Campbell gave another disappointing performance in the second debate. Charest was declared the winner once again. Campbell played it safe and refused to take a stand on Bill 178, the Quebec law that bans English from commercial signs. In contrast, Charest stood by his federalist principles and said repeatedly that Quebec should be more tolerant of its English-speaking minority. Columnist Jeffrey Simpson wrote that Charest showed himself to be a "model of statesmanship, alive to principle, aware of political reality." Throughout the debate

Campbell read from prepared notes that had been drafted by ardent Quebec nationalists in her camp. Describing the province as a distinct society, she rejected "centralizing and domineering federalism," echoing the exact words that Premier Robert Bourassa had used during the constitutional negotiations.

Two days earlier, Campbell appeared to endorse the "notwithstanding" clause that had been used by Quebec to enforce its discriminatory language laws. "I come from a province that was responsible for the 'notwithstanding' clause. . . . I understand why it is there," she said. Her support for the constitutional override and her waffling on minority language rights stirred up fierce criticism. "Ms. Campbell is not some foreigner visiting Quebec," said the Montreal *Gazette*. "She aspires to be the prime minister of all Canadians, including Quebeckers. The prime minister of Canada does not legislate in provincial jurisdictions, but he or she does have a profound duty to exercise moral leadership."

As unfavorable articles began to roll off the presses, Campbell's organization became increasingly inept at handling reporters. Her campaign tours received minimal coverage partly because journalists had enormous difficulty finding out where she was going. Communications adviser Cindy Boucher, who had been brought aboard to deal with the media, often failed to return journalists' phone calls—a mortal sin in a business geared to deadlines. Although a new press secretary was eventually hired to rebuild relations with the media, he proved to be no match for the spin doctors in Charest's camp.

Team Tortoise understood the need to have the media onside. Jodi White recruited two former opponents—Tim Ralfe and Pat MacAdam—to function as masters of the spin. Ralfe, a former CBC reporter, had worked as a communications adviser to Joe Clark and, like White, had lived through the trench warfare of the 1983 battle for the leadership; MacAdam, a former lobbyist, served as Mulroney's chief hatchet man against Clark in the early

1980s. Every day, Ralfe worked the phones and cozied up to reporters over drinks at the National Press Club bar. He and MacAdam made sure that journalists were well informed about all of Campbell's shortcomings, difficulties and mistakes.

Confident of victory, Campbell's advisers ignored Charest's dirty-tricks squad and failed to appoint competent professionals to deal with key people in the media. It was a strategic blunder that Ray Castelli and Ross Reid tried to correct late in the campaign by assigning the task to Brian McInnes and Justin de Beauchamp, two respected experts in communications.

Delegate selection meetings began the day after the second debate. One-quarter of the 3,846 eligible delegates were ex-officios—MPs, senators, provincial members and top brass of the party. These 966 unelected Tories outnumbered the regular and youth delegates elected in Nova Scotia, New Brunswick and all four western provinces. If Campbell could maintain her position as frontrunner, she could expect to attract at least half of the ex-officios to her side. Although the remaining delegates were up for grabs, Campbell's large organization gave her an edge in the contest for their votes. Because she was so well financed and well staffed, she was able to recruit thousands of new members to vote for her slates of delegates in advance of the selection process.

Charest resolved to outmuscle Campbell in his home province despite his lack of money and the help she was receiving from the party establishment. Fortunately, he had help from Pierre Claude Nolin, a crafty Mulroney organizer. The 42-year-old Nolin, whom Mulroney named to the Senate as one of his last acts as prime minister, was matched against Jean-Yves Lortie, a millionaire Montreal bailiff who was also one of Mulroney's political fixers. Although Lortie was a superb organizer, he was handicapped by overconfidence. When the voting for delegates got under way, Lortie departed to Florida for a vacation with his girlfriend. Nolin was left with a clear playing field.

Neither Pierre Blais nor Gilles Loiselle had the experience to take on Nolin, who quickly recruited new Tories to stack the meetings. At one meeting in Montreal, a group of Haitian immigrants turned up to vote for a Charest slate because they thought he hailed from Haiti. "I believe that because [Charest] is a Haitian like us, he'll be better able to help us out in our crisis," one man said. Nolin managed to garner 55 percent of the delegates in the first week of selection. Near the end of the campaign, Charest was ahead of Campbell in Quebec by a margin of two to one.

Charest also gained ground on the national stage. He won endorsements from Barbara McDougall, Bill McKnight and Public Works Minister Elmer MacKay, a strong player in the Maritimes. By May 8, when the final delegates' meetings were concluded, Charest had reason to be optimistic. Although Campbell had won 45 percent of the delegates compared with his 27 percent, Charest knew that 15 to 17 percent of the delegates were uncommitted. He still had a chance to win.

Campbell's confidence was given a boost in Calgary during the third TV debate. Minutes before the debate started, Bernard Valcourt, a close friend of Charest's and a powerbroker in New Brunswick, declared that he would support Campbell. The announcement was clearly designed to knock Charest off his stride. It worked. Charest seemed ill at ease, while a self-assured Campbell was crisp and precise.

Back in Ottawa, Campbell moved quickly to capitalize on her strong performance. Michael Wilson, the darling of the party's right wing, endorsed her when he became convinced that she was invincible. Campbell immediately called on delegates to give her a first-ballot victory. "I think given the fact that we will be in an election very soon after this leadership, I think for the unity of the party it would be very good to have a first-ballot victory." The presumptuousness revealed in this request was matched by Campbell's strategists, who told *Maclean's* the names of her cabinet and announced that the election would be called in the first week after Labour Day.

Campbell's image was eroding in the mind of the public even though the candidate herself felt confident. In mid-May, a Gallup poll showed that Charest had made sharp inroads among the electorate at Campbell's expense. In early April she had been favored by 51 percent of respondents compared to 15 percent for Charest; the new poll revealed that Campbell's support had dropped to 38 percent, while Charest's had risen to 31 percent.

On May 13, Joe Clark made a bizarre pronouncement: he declared that he might enter the race at the eleventh hour. His closest supporters had advised him against making such a ridiculous move, but he resented Campbell because of her interference in the constitutional talks and still dreamed of having one more dance with power. Hoping to be drafted by an enthusiastic group of fans, Clark quickly discovered that no one wanted him to run. When he bowed out the next day, he left the impression that there was profound unease with Campbell's candidacy.

Campbell's slide in popularity had a lot to do with the avalanche of opposition attacks upon her, with the intense media scrutiny she was receiving and with her uneven performances in the debates. Her tendency to make verbal gaffes also had a negative effect. She uttered her first major controversial statement at the end of the fourth debate, in Vancouver, when she lashed out at Canadians who oppose Tory economic policies. "The enemies of Canadians . . . are those people who are telling Canadians that debt and deficits are not a problem," she said. "Those are the people we have to take on in the next election." Moments after she uttered the fateful words, she scrambled to retract them, saying she had used the word *enemies* "mildly." But the damage had been done.

All her efforts to sound like a new age "inclusive" politician were wiped out by that single statement. Canadians were reminded of Mulroney's highly partisan remark during the 1992 referendum campaign, when he labelled Quebec nationalists "enemies of Canada." Campbell's words inspired reporters to conjure up her image as an elitist as they harked back to her days in Vancouver politics. Charest seized the opportunity to portray himself as the more tolerant candidate. "Obviously people who don't agree with our ideas are as Canadian as we are," he said. "They have a right to disagree."

Campbell's campaign suffered a severe blow on May 18, the day of the final TV debate. Tim Ralfe gave press gallery reporters copies of a profile of Campbell in the May issue of *Vancouver Magazine*. Written by Peter C. Newman, the piece was generally flattering, but it did reveal some hard edges to Campbell's personality. Newman, a close friend of Mulroney's and his official biographer, had invited the minister of Defence to a three-hour lunch at the elegant Empress Hotel in Victoria. The icon of Canadian journalism planned to test Campbell's reputation for being irreverent and outspoken. Ever willing to please, Campbell was humorous, forthcoming and blunt throughout their conversation.

Near the end of the interview, Campbell spoke about the problem of apathy in Canadian politics. Her words implied that only political partisans could qualify as responsible citizens. "The thing that infuriates me is apathy," she said. "People who boast about how they've never been involved in a political party. . . Who do they think is working to keep this society intact so they can have the luxury of sitting back and being such condescending SOBs? To hell with them."

Newman also reported other comments in which Campbell displayed her tendency to hold others in contempt. She dismissed Clark's come-from-behind win at the 1976 leadership convention as a "technical feat." Clark, she explained, had won because he "was the least-hated candidate." This was certainly true, but it was an unwise description of a man as well liked as Joe Clark. Campbell's remark was also unlikely to win much favor with the prime minister, since her comment implied that Mulroney, who had lost to Clark in 1976, was even more unpopular with the delegates.

Reporter Patrick Doyle recognized the news value in Newman's article and claimed the front page of *The Toronto Star* with a story about Campbell's sharp tongue. He took three additional quotes out of context. According to Doyle, Campbell boasted that she spoke fluent Yiddish, said that she had memorized all the books of the Bible and explained that she became an Anglican "as a way of warding off the evil demons of the papacy." Thus, Campbell à la Doyle appeared to be a conceited, puffed-up braggart who was anti-Catholic to boot.

Without reading either Newman's article or the transcript on which it was based, journalists accepted Doyle's version of Campbell's comments. CTV's "Canada AM," CBC's "Newsworld," CBC national radio and countless radio stations credulously repeated the *Star*'s account. In fact, both Newman's piece and Doyle's gloss on it appear to distort what Campbell said. The transcript of the conversation reveals that all three of Campbell's seemingly outrageous remarks about religion are quite innocuous in context.

> "I wasn't raised in a preachy environment—my own parents were not particularly religious at all; they encouraged my sister and me to make our own discoveries. I had a friend who went to a Pentecostal church and I went to Sunday school with her for a couple of years. I can still recite the books of the Bible and sing all sorts of rousing hymns. When I went to St. Ann's, which is a convent school in Victoria, it was pre-Vatican II days, the nuns still wore the habit, the mass was in Latin. I became a confirmed Anglican the year I was there, I suppose to ward off the evil demons of the papacy, given I was brought up in a basically Scot Presbyterian family. My father, in fact, was raised partly by a Catholic foster father so my father had been Catholic for a while but by the time he met my mother he had left the Church. And, of course, my first husband was Jewish. I speak the best Yiddish of any Gentile west of New York!"

Campbell was compelled to call a news conference a few hours before the TV debate to respond to the furor created by the article in the *Star*. In a frantic effort at damage control, her campaign team distributed copies of Newman's profile to delegates and reporters. For the first time in nearly a month, Campbell received favorable media coverage on the evening newscasts and in the next day's papers. Newspaper columnists and editorialists described her as performing well in the debate and condemned the *Star*'s piece as a hatchet job. "Sleazy, sleazy journalism," wrote columnist William Johnson in the Montreal *Gazette*. "*The Toronto Star* and the three electronic media owe Kim Campbell a full retraction and apology for the irresponsible way in which they assassinated her character."

But later that week Campbell was in trouble again. During a campaign stopover in Quebec City, a journalist asked her to comment on a month-old news story that revealed she had once smoked marijuana while at university. Campbell asserted that she had not broken the law when she puffed on the joint. Toronto criminal lawyer Clayton Ruby quickly disabused the former Justice minister of the notion that smoking grass was legal, and Campbell had to apologize for yet another gaffe. "I'm not experienced," she said. "I don't deal with drug prosecutions. If Clayton Ruby thinks I narrowly escaped jail, well, he must be right because he does criminal law."

All the blunders and controversy dramatically affected Campbell's popularity with the Canadian public. An Angus Reid poll published on May 22 marked a change in the dynamics of the campaign. Charest, the former underdog, was now judged to be the only Tory leader capable of defeating the Liberals. Reid found that 37 percent of Canadians would vote for a Charest-led party, compared with 31 percent who would back one headed by Campbell. Another survey, published in Quebec City's *Le Soleil*, identified Charest as the only Conservative leader who could win more votes in Quebec than the separatist Bloc Québécois. "Winnability" was slipping away from Kim Campbell.

Insisting that the survey was skewed because it had been done immediately after the uproar caused by Newman's article, Campbell claimed that she was still doing well. "I'm getting strong support from delegates," she said. "In fact, if the poll were to be taken today you'd get quite a different result." But Norman Atkins, a wise backroom strategist, was not quite as sanguine. The controversies had "shaken the confidence of delegates," he warned.

Charest's advisers were jubilant. Their plan to steal Campbell's lead had succeeded. Now their candidate appeared more likely to give the Tories what they wanted: victory in the next election. David Small of Team Tortoise knew that winning was uppermost in the minds of most delegates: "Brian Mulroney was so successful in 1983 at whetting the appetites of Tories for power. They do not want to lose that. The reason why so many delegates are soft or uncommitted so late in the exercise is because they wanted to be absolutely sure that on the issue of winnability they were making the right decision."

One week before the convention, panic swept Campbell's camp. A Compas survey of Tory delegates for *The Financial Post* and the Toronto *Sun* newspaper chain concluded that she had only a 5 percent lead over Charest among the delegates. Furthermore, her second-ballot support was soft, and a staggering 68 percent of those polled judged her to be "unstable and unpredictable" while 45 percent found her "arrogant." Compas concluded that Charest had the greatest potential for growth on a second ballot, since he could count on 73 percent of Jim Edwards's delegates to join him after the first round of voting.

Shocked by the survey, Campbell went on the attack for the first time in the campaign. She hurriedly arranged interviews with major news outlets and portrayed Charest as a lightweight: not only had he resigned from cabinet for phoning a judge but he had passed only four bills in his eight years at the cabinet table. Doug Lewis, Ontario chairman of Campbell's campaign, ordered MPs to get on the phones to shore up support, and Ian Anderson, an Ottawa consultant and tough backroom player, was brought in to put Campbell's camp in order. Paul Curley, a Toronto consultant and former national party director, set to work orchestrating a skilled team of handlers for the convention.

Over the June 4–5 weekend there were signs that the tide was beginning to turn in Campbell's favor. A Canadian Press survey of delegates found that Campbell still had a comfortable lead over Charest, although she was considerably short of a first-ballot victory. A poll by Angus Reid for CTV and *Maclean's*, which showed Campbell leading Charest at 43 percent to 31 percent, suggested that Campbell was within close reach of winning on the first ballot if she could hang on to her committed delegates and win one out of every four of the 15 percent who were still undecided.

Charest's strategy to garner the favor of the uncommitted delegates and those who were "soft" supporters of Campbell was simple and direct: discredit Campbell, allay worries about his youth and Quebec roots, build momentum and stress his "winnability."

For nearly two months Charest had contrasted his status as a family man with that of Campbell's as a childless, twice-divorced woman. His wife, Michèle, who styles herself after Mila Mulroney, accompanied him everywhere and chirped about their high-school romance, early marriage and three beautiful children. Once the Compas poll showed that some delegates thought Campbell was unstable, Charest's partisans played up their candidate's solid family life. "Together Jean and Michèle, as the parents of three young children, have a personal stake in the country's future," said Maureen McTeer, noted feminist and wife of Joe Clark, when she endorsed Charest a week before the convention. Tory MP Terry Clifford used the same logic: "Clearly, someone who has a family—that they have to look after—has got a commitment to other people that have families, and I think it's part of why people can identify with Charest."

Throughout the campaign Charest used charm and wit to counter the charge that he was too young to be prime minister. When Andy Saxton, a 29-year-old Campbell supporter running in Vancouver Quadra, posed a question, Charest remarked that "I hope nobody ever told you you're too young."

"I'm getting older and wiser all the time," replied Saxton.

"Join the club, Andy, join the club," said the tortoise.

A series of announcements from prominent Tories who had switched to Charest gave his campaign a boost. A group of key party figures, including Harry Near, Jim Ramsay, consultant Elizabeth Roscoe and backroomer George Stratton, declared for Charest days before the convention started. The biggest news came on June 6, when Joe Clark publicly endorsed him. Two days later Fisheries Minister John Crosbie went to Charest, followed by minister of state for Finance John McDermid. In previous weeks he had won the backing of several of Mulroney's close associates: Senator Michel Cogger, Brian Gallery, former Newfoundland premier Frank Moores, Luc Lavoie and Bernard Roy. This procession appeared to indicate that Mulroney himself had concluded Charest was the better choice.

In fact, Mulroney had privately informed friends that he had made a "mistake" in thinking that Campbell could win the election against the Liberals. "He's been bad-mouthing her," one close friend told the *Sun* newspapers. "He said 'it's been in a free fall since March.' He was extremely critical of her and he was very laudatory and complimentary to Charest." Mulroney hit the roof when his comments were reported. His press secretary called the story "an absolute lie." But Mulroney, who knew the *Sun*'s source, did not reprimand his friend for leaking their conversation. The surest sign that the prime minister favored Charest came on the day of the vote, when Hugh Segal endorsed the kid from Sherbrooke.

A few last-minute slips undermined Charest's careful strategy. First, the usually cautious Bill McKnight warned Campbell's supporters that they were courting suicide in the election if their candidate became the leader. He compared them to the 900 followers of cult leader Jim Jones who drank poisoned Kool-Aid in 1978. McKnight refused to retract his remark, and Charest appeared to be ungracious when he stopped short of demanding that his supporter apologize to Campbell.

Charest stumbled again by suggesting that he might not serve in a Campbell-led government. Since Campbell said she would be happy to work in Charest's cabinet, Charest's hesitation made him seem like a spoiled brat who was threatening to go home if he did not win the prize.

In the final days of the contest, Campbell stressed the importance of choosing a woman to head the party. "This campaign I'm involved in represents change," she told CTV. "It represents reaching out and broadening the base of the party, and maybe some people are uncomfortable with that." According to Tory legend, Flora MacDonald lost the 1976 Tory leadership race because of her gender. When MacDonald gave Campbell a moving, eloquent endorsement, the symbolism was not lost on delegates: they were being asked to disprove the longstanding notion that the Tory party is anti-woman.

In the end, criticism of the tactics used by Team Tortoise and skilful use of the gender factor stalled Charest's momentum and breathed new life into Campbell's campaign. At the convention, she performed well in two policy debates where she wooed pro-family delegates by promising to reduce the level of violence on television and by speaking affectionately about her three stepdaughters from her marriage to Nathan Divinsky.

Campbell's team superbly tracked each and every delegate. Those who were soft or uncommitted were targeted by senior ministers such as Beatty, Lewis, Valcourt and Wilson. Bob Horner, chair of the Commons Justice Committee, and Scott

Newark, head of the Canadian Police Association, went after delegates concerned with law and order. In the days leading up to the vote, Campbell met with about 400 delegates in groups of 15 to 20. Besides functioning smoothly, her organization looked impressive in the stadium; supporters wearing pink "Kim" caps seemed to be everywhere.

On Friday, June 11, two days before the voting, the media fired another round at Campbell by releasing a week-old Gallup poll that predicted "electoral disaster" for the Tories under Campbell but a comfortable majority government with Charest. The announcement of this highly speculative prophecy of doom, printed in *The Toronto Star*, appeared to have been timed to have the greatest influence on undecided delegates. Tory pollster Allan Gregg accused Gallup of being "unprofessional" by "explicitly" imploring delegates to vote for Charest.

Most observers felt that Charest triumphed in the battle of the candidates' speeches on the Saturday night. In a classic address to the convention, he enthralled the delegates by attacking the opposition parties and pledging an electoral win. Speaking easily and eloquently, he delivered one of the best speeches of his political career. Campbell's entrance was much more dramatic as her supporters thronged the stage, waving their pink-and-white campaign signs, but her speech was surprisingly flat. In trying to project a prime ministerial image with a speech that was supposed to demonstrate substance over style, she failed to ignite the audience. The most effective moment of her presentation occurred when Ellen Fairclough, Canada's first female federal cabinet minister, introduced her. There was still no clear winner going into the final day.

On Sunday, June 13, Ottawa's Civic Centre was a political pressure cooker. Feelings were running high and media speculation was intense. Opinion about who would be the victor was equally divided when the delegates lined up in the sweltering heat to cast their ballots for the leader of their party and Canada's nineteenth prime minister. When the results of the first ballot were announced, Campbell was within 71 votes of victory, with a total of 1,664; Charest was second with 1,369. Campbell had 48 percent of the magic number needed to win; victory was within her reach. Patrick Boyer, Jim Edwards and Garth Turner dropped out after the first ballot, leaving only the hare and the tortoise in the race. When Edwards surprisingly crossed the floor to sit in Campbell's box, it was all over. His support guaranteed that a sufficient number of the 307 delegates who had voted for him would cast their ballots for Campbell in the second round. The final tally gave Campbell a slim majority over Charest: 1,817 delegates or 52.7 percent to 1,630 or 47.3 percent. Some of Charest's supporters wept openly at the results, and a stony-faced Joe Clark watched as the candidates made their way to the platform. Kim Campbell had beaten the odds, after all.

Although Campbell won the leadership, many agreed with pollster Conrad Winn that Charest won the "gold medal for campaign success." The tortoise outperformed and outdebated the hare and offered Canadians a stronger federalist vision of their nation. Campbell's gaffes demonstrated that she was no political messiah; the next election would be an interesting one.

Campbell was victorious because she had learned a hard political lesson from her unsuccessful bid for the Socred leadership in 1986: she knew that she needed a strong team to win. Well before the delegates were selected, she assembled a national organization that, despite its flaws, helped her withstand the attacks of Charest's troops, kept her delegates in line even when polls showed she would lose to the Liberals, and controlled the convention floor.

But Campbell has other lessons to learn. If she is to enjoy future victories, she will have to curb her inclination to be disdainful of her adversaries. In her victory speech, she gave little more than a curt acknowledgment to Charest as he stood onstage, exhausted and forlorn, beside his weeping wife. "Jean, I don't know whether I'm a rabbit or not, but you're one hell of a tortoise," she quipped, sending a wave of resentment rippling through the large contingent of Charest's supporters. For many viewers, her comments contrasted sharply with the eloquence of Iona Campagnolo, whose praise of Jean Chrétien, at the moment of his defeat by John Turner for the Liberal leadership, is still remembered.

Kim Campbell has attained her childhood dream of becoming prime minister. She has made history by becoming both the first woman and the first British Columbian to hold the highest office in the land. Canadians have seen her colorful personality, her flashes of brilliance and her penchant for turning a memorable phrase. She has also proven to be certain of her opinions and calm in the face of controversy. In our era, when images crumble so quickly and leaders disappoint so easily, she will be challenged to use her unusual qualities to inspire Canadians with a sense of optimism and purpose that is neither divisive nor ephemeral.

SELECTED
BIBLIOGRAPHY

Broadfoot, Anne. *Victoria and Vancouver Island. A Pictorial Tour of Beautiful Vancouver Island and Victoria, Capital City of the Province of British Columbia*. Vancouver: Spectrum Enterprises, 1970.

Garr, Allen. *Tough Guy: Bill Bennett and the Taking of British Columbia*. Toronto: Key Porter Books, 1985.

Greer, Rosamond "Fiddy." *The Girls of the King's Navy*. Victoria, B.C.: Sono Nis Press, 1983.

Kilian, Crawford. *School Wars: The Assault on B.C. Education*. Vancouver: New Star Books, 1985.

Kirk, Russell. *The Conservative Mind: From Burke to Eliot*. Chicago: Regnery Books, 1986.

Leslie, Graham. *Breach of Promise: Socred Ethics Under Vander Zalm*. Madeira Park, B.C.: Harbour Publishing Co., 1991.

Martin, Lawrence. *Pledge of Allegiance: The Americanization of Canada in the Mulroney Years*. Toronto: McClelland & Stewart, 1993.

Mason, Gary and Keith Baldrey. *Fantasyland: Inside the Reign of Bill Vander Zalm*. Toronto: McGraw-Hill Ryerson, 1989.

Murray, Peter. *From Amor to Zalm: A Primer on B.C. Politics and its Wacky Premiers*. Victoria, B.C.: Orca Book Publishers, 1989.

Persky, Stan. *Fantasy Government: Bill Vander Zalm and the Future of Social Credit*. Vancouver: New Star Books, 1989.

Roy, Reginald H. *The Seaforth Highlanders, 1919–1965*. Vancouver: Evergreen Press, 1969.

Schapiro, Leonard B. *The Communist Party of the Soviet Union*. London: Eyre & Spottiswoode, 1960.

Schapiro, Leonard B., ed. *Political Opposition in One-Party States*. New York: John Wiley & Sons, 1972.

Twigg, Alan. *Vander Zalm: From Immigrant to Premier*. Madeira Park, B.C.: Harbour Publishing Co., 1986.

INDEX